Letters

FROM THE

Smokies

BY MICHAEL ADAY

WITH DENISE ADAY

There are more than a million documents in the archives of Great Smoky Mountains National Park. Lucky for us, Michael Aday has culled a selection of some of the most fascinating, the earliest being a writ issued in 1785 from the short-lived State of Franklin and the latest a 20th-century protest over bear-management policies. Within that three-century span, Aday captures stories of people whose voices we don't often hear. Letters from the Smokies *is a delight to read!*

~ Janet McCue, librarian emerita, Cornell University, and coauthor of *Back of Beyond: A Horace Kephart Biography*

❧

Letters from the Smokies *breathes life into the tense, sometimes tenuous experiences that come with living close to the land during times of uncertainty and oppression. Spanning over two centuries of correspondence, the letters are at turns curious, surprising, and tragic. Aday's dexterity at explaining the context surrounding the letters turns compelling actions and decisions into unforgettable narratives of Appalachia's economic, cultural, and political issues. An essential addition to the bookshelves of those who love and appreciate the region.*

~ Latria Graham, 2019 Steve Kemp Writer-in-Residence, journalist and assistant professor, Augusta University

❧

This imaginative book offers letters from famous and not-so-famous people whose lives were in some manner or other intertwined with the history of the Great Smoky Mountains. Aday's commentaries are concise, clear, well-focused, and pleasingly informative. More importantly, they have the capacity to spark within the enlightened reader an urge to know more and perhaps delve further into the history of the Smokies.

~ Ken Wise, professor emeritus, University of Tennessee, and author of *Hiking Trails of the Great Smoky Mountains*

Perfect for the curious park visitor or history buff, Letters from the Smokies *is a carefully curated testimony to the power of archival collections to inform and humanize the historical record. Each document is accompanied by a well-written essay placing the archival item within the history of the Smokies region. Taken together, the essays illuminate the ways that people have interacted with the land and with each other to create the national park as it exists today.*

    ~ Anne Bridges, retired University of Tennessee librarian and co-author
       of *Terra Incognita: An Annotated Bibliography of the Great Smoky Mountains,*
       1544–1934 and *The Terra Incognita Reader: Early Writings from the Great*
       Smoky Mountains

℘

Letters *reveals the complexity of the Smokies' history through the voices of those who lived it. It captures residents' struggles for survival as well as the intentions of those who shaped the national park. Readers learn of consequential losses, conflicts, and achievements in present tense, as events unfold, before outcomes are known. These vignettes enrich our experience of the Great Smoky Mountains.*

    ~ Elizabeth Giddens, PhD, Professor of English, Kennesaw State University, and
       author of *Oconaluftee: The History of a Smoky Mountain Valley*

Edited by Frances Figart

Editorial assistance by Aaron Searcy

Book design and production by Karen Key

All images reproduced courtesy of Great Smoky Mountains National Park archives
unless otherwise noted.

Printed in Birmingham, Alabama

ISBN: 978-0-937207-25-3

1   2   3   4   5   6   7   8   9   10

Published by Great Smoky Mountains Association.

Great Smoky Mountains Association is a nonprofit organization that supports the educational, scientific, and historical programs of Great Smoky Mountains National Park. Our publications are an educational service intended to enhance the public's understanding and enjoyment of the national park. To learn more about our publications, memberships, and projects, visit SmokiesInformation.org or call 865.436.7318.

For those

WHO CALL THE GREAT
SMOKY MOUNTAINS HOME—
IN BODY OR IN SPIRIT

Author's Note

The idea for *Letters from the Smokies* began with a suggestion from my wife over Sunday morning coffee in 2019. She was reading the book *Letters of Note: Correspondence Deserving of a Wider Audience* compiled by Shaun Usher. This fascinating collection of letters from famous and not-so-famous people reveals deeper stories about the correspondents and their times.

As is her habit, Denise read aloud some that she found most interesting. Then she looked at me and said, "You should write something like this from letters in the park archives."

What a brilliant idea!

As the archivist at Great Smoky Mountains National Park, I have access to nearly 1.4 million historic documents: thousands of pages of government correspondence covering decades of park service management decisions; reams of letters documenting the herculean task of establishing the park; and hundreds of documents chronicling the lives of many of those who lived here before the park existed.

I quickly realized the genuine challenge would not be what to put in but what to leave out!

After several weeks perusing collections and making copious lists, I finally whittled the selection down to the 19 documents in this volume. While these chapters can't tell the entire story of an area as vast and a history as deep as that of the Smokies, I hope they bring a unique perspective and scope.

Although any archival collection represents the entity it documents, it also reflects the social power structures in place over a period of time. If the dominant narrative is White and male, that tends to influence the way collections are cataloged, arranged, and described.

The original inhabitants of the Smokies are the Cherokee people, who still live and thrive in this region. I wanted to include stories about their contributions to the history of the mountains but this proved to be a challenge. Few Cherokee-related records exist within the park's collection, and what does exist requires further scholarship and interpretation in collaboration with the Eastern Band of Cherokee Indians. I hope a future edition can include their voices and material.

If nothing else, this project has allowed me to uncover a few singular artifacts within the archive that have been largely overlooked. It is my hope that these letters and their stories will give readers a deeper appreciation of the Smokies. While some stories will be known to many, I endeavored to present new and interesting ones and to bring fresh perspective to those that are familiar.

I was constantly awed by the stories I found in the archives. The audacity of people like David Chapman and Jack Huff astounded me. To this day I can't talk about Deborah McGee without choking up. Some made me laugh out loud, some made me angry or sad . . . and some hopeful. But they all made me grateful to be the archivist for Great Smoky Mountains National Park.

Thank you for reading. ❧

Michael Aday

Acknowledgments

There has been one abiding passion throughout my life—history. My interest began in second grade with the Michael Caine film *Zulu*. The movie captivated my imagination and spawned a lifelong fascination with the history of our world.

While my own natural curiosity served me well for many years, it wasn't until I went back to college with an eye toward becoming a history professor that I began to study in earnest. Although my career path veered from the anticipated trajectory, I wouldn't be where I am now without the kindness and support of many people. Though I can't thank all of them here, I would like to acknowledge some who were crucial to my development. Dr. Kyle Wilkison, Dr. Joan Jenkins, Dr. David Cullen, and Dr. Sam Tullock encouraged my scholarly pursuits, even after I chose a different path. Their honesty, kindness, and friendship can never be repaid.

Over the years, I have worked in several museums and archives. At each one, I was fortunate to know some amazing people who mentored and guided me to become the professional I am today. Sam Childers, Ross Crabtree, John Slate, Evelyn Montgomery, Brenna Lissoway, Mary Gentry, Jackie Zak, and John McDade provided me with indispensable advice, friendship, humor, and support. Thank you.

Though all the documents in this book came from the park archives, it would have been irresponsible for me to rely solely on my own expertise to interpret their meaning and place them in a broader context. I was fortunate to find so many people willing to answer questions and provide additional insight into the stories explored in this book. With deep gratitude I wish to thank Alex McKay and the staff of the Haywood County Historical and Genealogical Society; Elizabeth Avery Thomas; Kirk Savage; Jennie Holy Haynes and the staff at Old Fort Genealogy; Becky Arrants; Dr. Edward M. Burns of the Carl Van Vechten Trust; Julie Webb; Don Casada; and Maria Ferguson of the Roger Tory Peterson Institute.

I would also like to thank the outstanding creative services team at Great Smoky Mountains Association. Frances Figart, Aaron Searcy, and Karen Key have been patient, enthusiastic supporters of this project from the beginning. Their expertise, creativity, and attention to detail are astonishing.

Thank you to Stephanie Kyriazis, the chief of resource education for Great Smoky Mountains National Park, for her thoughtful reading and insightful comments on the book.

And finally, this book would have been impossible without my wife, Denise. Not only did she suggest the idea, but she also guided me through each chapter—clarifying, challenging, smoothing, and polishing. She knew which questions to ask when I couldn't find my way through a forest of confusion. She helped me see sense when I wanted to chuck the entire project and reigned me in when I strayed too far afield. The qualities that have made her amazing in our marriage make her an outstanding editor, too. ☙

Contents

Introduction

The National Park Service is known for protecting landscapes with dramatic vistas, stewarding vital ecosystems, and maintaining structures where historically significant events unfolded. These efforts are readily visible to anyone experiencing national parks in person or virtually. Yet the agency is also responsible for a lesser-known form of preservation that takes place behind the scenes.

The Great Smoky Mountains National Park archives contain 1.4 million documents, while the museum collections house 235,000 objects. These precious bits of material— from pressed flowers to extinct birds, from nostalgic notes to the pen that signed the Smokies into park status—offer hidden details about the natural and cultural history of a place beloved by millions of people.

Although carefully organized and ensconced in climate-controlled rooms, these collections are not off limits to the public. With pre-scheduled appointments, scientists, history scholars, and family genealogists alike are welcome to access documents or objects of interest. Yet with so many scraps of history to choose from, the casually curious Smokies lover might not know where to start.

Luckily, the park's archivist, Mike Aday, has thoughtfully curated this fascinating collection of writings that highlight the breadth of the Smokies narrative. This book offers an enticing entrée into the deep and diverse Southern Appalachian world that has unfolded around what we now call Great Smoky Mountains National Park.

In these ancient mountains, humans have intersected and entangled for millennia. Several of the letters in this book explore these complex and complicated relationships.

A letter documenting debt payment rendered through the sale of enslaved people reminds readers that the mountains were not free from the scourge of human bondage.

A travel pass issued to Cades Cove resident Elijah Oliver by the US Army highlights the tensions and flux of eastern Tennessee during the Civil War. The state seceded, despite overwhelming pro-Union sentiment in the eastern third, but US troops liberated Knoxville and surrounding areas beginning in 1863, controlling the movement of residents both loyal and Confederate until the end of the war.

A contract of indentured servitude between two newly freed people of color complicates the narrative around emancipation—though legally liberated, the formerly enslaved had to forge new lives with few resources in often hostile white communities. The persistence of this inequity is echoed in a letter from 1926 showing that, while many local Black folks financially supported the establishment of Great Smoky Mountains National Park, this "public land" maintained segregated facilities until the 1950s.

While many of the letters in this book illuminate heavy historical moments, others offer lighter fare. Readers can revel in the mountain moxie of women like writer Mary Noailles Murfree, best-selling author of "local color" tales from the hol-

lers, or Waynesville postmaster and (licensed) liquor entrepreneur Deborah McGee. There are limericks composed during a freezing night on Mount Le Conte and the letter that accompanied the Smokies bobcat gifted to President Coolidge.

Road-tripping scientists, perennial park management issues, early tourism, and letters longing for a far-away mountain home all feature in these pages. These stories, and more than a million others, reside permanently preserved in the archives of Great Smoky Mountains National Park.

Perhaps this chorus of voices will entice you to dig deeper into the history of the mountains. Or perhaps these letters will inspire you to write your own page of the Smokies story and, thus, contribute to the colorful future of a place bursting with diversity of life!

~ Stephanie Kyriazis
NPS Chief of Resource Education
Great Smoky Mountains National Park

Early Documents of the
Great Smoky Mountains

1785 – 1879

State of Franklin

To the Sheriff of Washington &c

We Command you to take Joseph Young if in your bailwick and him safely keep so that you have him before the Justices of our County Court of pleas and quarter sessions to be held on the first monday in McCall next then and there to answer Alexander Denny In a plea of assault & Battery Damage five Hundred pounds Herein fail not and have you there this writ Witness James Sevier Clerke of our said court at office the first monday in february A.D. 178

Is. 7th febr 1786

James Sevier C. C.

Alexr Denny
vs
Joseph Young

Case B

to May. 1786

Executed on the Deffendant
Jas Alexr
Shff

Recd. Wm V. P.

1785

State of Franklin

To the Sheriff of Washington Co.
We command you to take Joseph Young if in your bailiwick and
him safely keep so that you have him before the justices of
our County Court of pleas and quarter sessions to be held
on the first monday in May next then and there to answer
Alexander Donny in a pleas of assault & Battery Damage five
hundred pounds. Herein fail not and have you there this writ
Witness James Sevier Clerke of our said Court at office the
first monday in february A.D. 178

Is. 7th february 1786
James Sevier C.C.

---

*This writ issued by James Sevier—son of the governor of Franklin—instructed the sheriff
of Washington County to take Joseph Young into custody in relation to a case of assault
and battery brought by Alexander Donny.*

$\mathcal{S}$oon after the end of the American Revolution, the newly formed nation faced an early crisis of continuity. Residents of four counties in Western North Carolina—Greene, Spencer, Sullivan, and Washington—voted to secede and form their own state.

Named Franklin in honor of American statesman Benjamin Franklin, this nascent body struggled to survive over the next four years against both internal and external threats. These events would foreshadow challenges the nation as a whole would face in the next century.

Portrait of Revolutionary War colonel John Sevier by James Wilson Peale. Image courtesy of Tennessee State Library and Archives.

To defray debts accrued during the revolution, the North Carolina legislature voted to yield control of the western portion of the state, modern-day Tennessee, to the newly formed federal government. Had the United States Congress accepted and approved the Cession Act of 1784, the general assembly would have given up claim to the "lands west of the Apalachians [*sic*] or Alleghany mountains [*sic*] . . . thence to the Mississippi." The act went on to stipulate that the land "shall be considered as a common fund for the use

and benefits . . . of the United States." In addition to ceding millions of acres, the act also nullified state treaties with Native Peoples.

White residents of the ceded Upper Tennessee Valley—approximately 5,000 people—felt betrayed and abandoned. Some worried that the cash-strapped nation would sell this new land to Spain or France. And they feared retaliatory violence from the Cherokee people, who had also been betrayed. Yet many of the officials representing Western North Carolina voted in favor of the act, seeing an opportunity to enrich themselves through land speculation. Between 1783 and 1784, members of the state legislature and their business associates claimed three million acres of land. One provision of the Cession Act guaranteed the validity of all existing land warrants under state law.

In August 1784, a meeting was held at Jonesborough, where the decision to secede and form a separate state was made. At a convention the following December, delegates affirmed their support for an independent state. They were unaware that in November the North Carolina legislature had rescinded the Cession Act, canceling their plans to jettison the western part of the state. In March 1785, a third convention was held. John Sevier was elected governor, and four new counties were established—Blount, Caswell, Sevier, and Wayne.

Sevier, a colonel in the American Revolution, was initially a reluctant supporter of the region's movement toward independence. He became an advocate once North Carolina Governor

An early 20th-century rendering of the boundary of the historic State of Franklin. Image courtesy of Tennessee State Library and Archives.

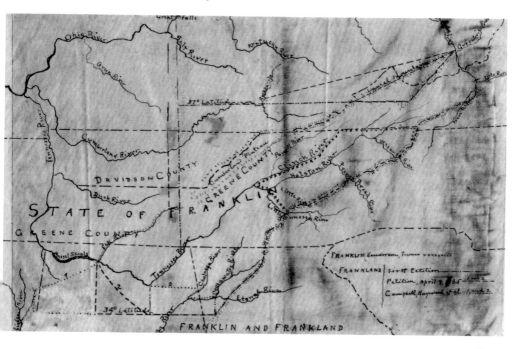

Alexander Martin issued a manifesto warning citizens of Franklin that "lesser causes have deluged states and kingdoms with blood." Martin went further, calling Sevier's support for statehood a "black and traitorous revolt."

To undermine the newly declared state, North Carolina established a parallel bureaucracy in the region. Each county had two governing bodies, two sheriffs, and two court systems operating simultaneously. The results were confusion, divided loyalties, and factional violence. This dual government forced residents of Franklin to register legal affairs, including marriages and land purchases, in both courts to ensure their legality. When faced with a choice between which entity to pay their taxes to, many took the middle ground and chose to pay neither state.

This writ issued by James Sevier—son of the governor of Franklin—instructed the sheriff of Washington County to take Joseph Young into custody in relation to a case of assault and battery brought by Alexander Donny. The particulars of the case are lost to the ages. The period when the writ was issued, however, encompasses a particularly tumultuous period in Franklin. The existence of a competing court system in the region devolved into a 'courthouse war,' punctuated by raids by both states on each other's courts,

complete with the theft of records and assaults on plaintiffs and officers of the court.

Matters came to a head in February 1788, when John Sevier was accused of tax delinquency and Col. John Tipton of the North Carolina militia ordered the seizure of Sevier's enslaved people as punishment. In response, Sevier marched his troops to Tipton's home on Sinking Creek, where a standoff lasting several days ensued. On February 29, reinforcements arrived from North Carolina. A brief skirmish followed, and Sevier withdrew his forces, ending the Battle of Franklin.

In August 1788, Sevier was arrested for treason. Earlier that year, to gain more land for Franklin, he had entered into an agreement with Spain. In exchange for a loan to help fund a war to steal land from the Chickamauga, Chickasaw, and other tribes, Franklin would be placed under Spanish rule. This was a step too far for North Carolina and resulted in Sevier's arrest. Though he escaped, in March 1789 Sevier and his remaining loyalists turned themselves in and swore oaths of loyalty to North Carolina—ending the State of Franklin.

Despite the failure of Franklin as a state movement, Sevier's star continued to rise. Between 1791 and his death in 1815, Sevier served in both the North Carolina and Tennessee state senates, two terms as governor of the newly formed state of Tennessee, and as a member of Congress.

Many historians refer to Franklin as "the lost state"—lost because it isn't widely known in our collective memory. Lost because it left behind none of the symbols of statehood recognized today—no capitol building or state flag. The only physical trace we have now is a handful of documents, scraps of paper nearly 250 years old. Though these records are irreplaceable, the tension they embody persists today in debates around local versus national control of law and property. ✌

State of No Carolina } To all to whom these shall
Haywood County } concern Know Ye, that
where as James R Love and myself have
become largely Indebted in the Merchantile
Buisneß which we have carried on for some
two or three years in the Town of Waynesville
Haywood County and in order that the debts
the said James R Love and the said R Love
may be honestly settled & fairly paid the said
Robert Love doth hereby agree that If the said
J R Love will sell a suffecient number of his
negros or slaves to pay off all of the above debts
dues and demands which may be owing
by the said Firm The said R Love on his part
agrees in as much as his negros are all of the
same family or relatives to convey to the
said Love by Bill a Sale or otherwise an equal
number of his negros or an equal number
in Value of those sold by the said
J R Love in payment of the said debts.
In Witneß where of J R Love here Unto
set my hand & seal 2th July 1833
                                    R Love {Seal}

Grievous to Posterity
Enslavement in Southern Appalachia

1830

———————

State of N. Carolina, Haywood County

To all to whom this shall concern know ye that where as
James R. Love and myself have become largely indebted in the
merchantile business which we have carried on for sime two
or three years in the Town of Waynesville Haywood County
and in order that the debts the said James R. Love and I the
said R. Love may be honestly settled and having paid the said
Robert Love doth hereby agree that if the said J.R. Love will
sell a sufficient number of his negros or slaves to pay off
all of the above debts due and demands which may be owing by
the said time the said R. Love on his part agrees in as much
as his negros are all of the same family or relatives to
convey to the J.R. Love by Bill of Sale or otherwise an equal
number of his negros or an equal number in value of those
sold by the said J.R. Love in paying off the said debts. In
where as where of I have here unto set my hand and seal 29th
July 1833.

R. Love (seal)

---

*In order to satisfy debts that James Love and his father Robert had accrued in an unspec-
ified mercantile venture, James agreed to "sell a sufficient number of his negroes or slaves
to pay off all of the above debts."*

There's a common misconception that the institution of slavery was relatively unknown in the mountains of Southern Appalachia. The absence of large-scale agriculture like that found in the Piedmont and the Delta has led some to think that the grassy balds and coves of the Great Smoky Mountains were free from this scourge.

The historic record, however, tells a different story. Enslaved African Americans were not only present in Southern Appalachia—they were integral to the region.

The Love family was one of the largest landowning families in Western North Carolina. Robert Love (1760–1845), a colonel in the American Revolution, was the founder of Waynesville, North Carolina. His son James Robert Love (1798–1863) served in the North Carolina legislature from 1821 to 1830. He and his father purchased vast tracts of land in Western North Carolina and East Tennessee that became part of the immense Love estate.

But business didn't always run smoothly. In order to satisfy debts that James and his father Robert had accrued in an unspecified mercantile venture, James agreed to "sell a sufficient number of his negroes or slaves to pay off all of the above debts." These casual words provide a brief view into the inhumane nature of American slavery.

The largest enslavers in Western North Carolina shared similar backgrounds; most were lawyers or politicians, and many were involved in the tourism industry. James Love, for example, owned a moderate farm and commercial business, was proprietor of the White Sulphur Springs Resort near Waynesville, and was Haywood County's largest enslaver.

Many of the people Love enslaved were used to cater to the needs of wealthy planters from South Carolina and Georgia that vacationed at his resort. The 1860 US Census Slave Schedule lists his holdings as 55 "slaves"

James Robert Love: landowner, politician, enslaver. Image courtesy of Alex McKay.

Turpentine harvesting in North Carolina. Enslaved labor was used to extract natural resources from the environment, including mining, logging, and as seen here, the harvesting of turpentine from pine trees. Image courtesy of slaveryimages.org

housed in ten buildings. Like his contemporaries in the agricultural areas of the Deep South, Love wielded great social and political influence.

Though there were numerous small- and medium-sized farms in the region, their agricultural output was insufficient to justify the use of enslaved labor on the same scale seen in other parts of either North Carolina or Tennessee. As a result, the percentage of enslaved people in the population of the western 15 counties of North Carolina never rose much above ten percent.

On a tour of the South for an 1854 series of articles on the evils of slavery, Frederick Law Olmstead noted that in Southern Appalachia "of the people who get their living entirely by agriculture few own negroes; the slaveholders being chiefly professional men, shop-keepers, and men in office." But slavery was still an element of life in Western North Carolina and reflected the economic and social status of White Carolinians.

Enslaved people were often leased by local residents for the skills they possessed. William Holland Thomas, an enslaver who operated a mercantile business in Quallatown and was an ally of the Cherokee people, rented one of John B. Love's enslaved people (unnamed in the documents) to operate a blacksmith shop for nearly a year.

In addition, stolen labor was used on public works projects such as the construction and maintenance of roads and public buildings. However, the largest use of enslaved Black people could be found in mining and railroad construction. Copper and gold mining in Western North Carolina and East Tennessee was one of the most profitable uses. The discovery of gold in Western North Carolina in 1828 resulted in a mining boom that affected several western counties until the mid-1850s. Enslaved labor made the exploitation of rare minerals more profitable than almost any other economic venture in the region.

It has been argued that enslaved people in the mountain highlands were subjected to less harsh treatment than their plantation counterparts. Olmstead noted of slavery in the region that its "moral evils are less, even less proportionately to the number of slaves."

It is true that enslaved African Americans laboring in the tourism industry had a larger degree of unrestricted movement than their counterparts in agriculture, mining, or logging. They often served as guides for visitors to the many resorts in the area. Having firsthand knowledge of the local terrain and conditions, they often independently led hunting and fishing expeditions.

While slavery in the mountains of Western North Carolina may not have followed the same pattern as in more agriculturally developed regions of the South, it was present, nonetheless. It was made integral to the regional economy, and enslavers in the highlands benefited from the elevated social status that 'owning another human being' seemingly conferred on their counterparts in the planter class.

Ultimately, any anecdotal evidence that treatment of enslaved Black people in the Smokies was less severe—evidence offered either by the enslavers themselves or from those viewing the system from the outside—does not change the fact that the system was abhorrent and brutal. That James Love and his father sold human beings to settle debt underscores the dehumanization at the heart of the institution of slavery. ✿

GOOD FOR ONE WEEK.

Provost Marshal's Office,

Knoxville, Tenn., *Oct 30* , 1863.

GUARDS will pass *Elijah Oliver*

Blue eyes, *light* hair, *4* feet *3* inches high, *35* years of age, *Fair* complexion, through the lines, on *Maryville* road.

J F Riddle

Capt. & Ass't. Provost Marshal.

Oath of Allegiance.

This Pass is given and taken with the condition that the bearer hereof solemnly swears to bear true faith and allegiance to the United States Government, and that he will conduct himself in all respects as a loyal citizen of said Government. For the faithful observance of this obligation he pledges his property and life.

His
Elijah X Oliver
mark

This pass was issued to Cades Cove, Tennessee, resident Elijah Oliver by the provost marshal in Knoxville. The pass allowed Oliver to travel through Union-occupied East Tennessee without fear of detention by federal troops.

The provost marshal was the military representative of the Union army and was responsible for maintaining civilian and military order in areas under federal occupation. These responsibilities included dealing with deserters, spies, and enemy prisoners. The provost also administered and recorded oaths of allegiance and controlled the movement of civilians in military zones.

To obtain an oath of allegiance, citizens had to offer proof of "sincerity and good faith" and be free of charges—civilian or criminal—before taking the oath.

Having satisfied the Union authorities of his loyalty, Oliver was issued passes that allowed him to travel from the cove to Maryville and Knoxville. He traveled to pay taxes and purchase medicine and household necessities like calico fabric, hair combs, and a coffee pot.

Faithful Observance
Elijah Oliver, Cades Cove, and the Civil War

1 8 6 3

———— *✧* ————

The Civil War was the most divisive, ruinous, and bloody event in 19th-century American history. Elijah Oliver and his neighbors in Cades Cove, Tennessee, knew this only too well. The bitterness and violence that tore the nation apart also engulfed this idyllic mountain valley.

Southern states began seceding in late 1860, with Tennessee joining in the spring of 1861. While much of the state embraced the call to secede, voters in the eastern portion resisted, preferring to remain loyal to the Union. Residents of the region went so far as to propose seceding from the Confederacy and forming their own pro-Union state.

What set East Tennessee apart from the rest of the state?

The economy and geography of the region accounted for part of the pro-Union sentiment. Large-scale agriculture that relied on the exploitation of enslaved labor was not feasible in much of the area, due in part to the distance from major rail terminals and other forms of reliable long-distance transportation. But Western North Carolina had much the same geography and economy and yet embraced enslavement and secession.

What East Tennessee had that other regions of the South did not was an active and vocal abolitionist

Knoxville, Tennessee 1864. *Confederate forces were driven from Knoxville in September 1863. From then until the end of the war the region was under control of Federal Provost Marshall, headquartered in Knoxville. Image courtesy of Library of Congress.*

movement, particularly strong in Blount County, where Cades Cove is located. As early as 1830, abolitionists in the area proposed establishing a separate state in order to abolish slavery. The county boasted a chapter of the Manumission Society of Tennessee dedicated to ending enslavement, and the town of Friendsville was founded by a group of Quakers who operated a way-station on the Underground Railroad.

The Reverend Isaac Anderson, founder of Maryville College, preached the gospel of abolition throughout the region and influenced many in this belief. His close friend from New York, Dr. Calvin Post, took up residence in Cades Cove as its only doctor and there shared his own abolitionist views.

Enslavement was not unknown to cove residents, however. Daniel Foute was one of the wealthiest, owning 20,000 acres, a forge, and mill. Foute had a vision for the economic development of the cove, including good roads to Knoxville and Maryville, as well as North Carolina. He hoped to draw entrepreneurs into the area to exploit natural resources such as iron, copper, and zinc. He also enslaved a number of people, though most lived in other areas of Blount County.

The 1850 and 1860 United States Census Slave Schedules do not list any enslaved people in the cove. In fact, the 1850 population census lists a free Black man, Cooper Clark, and a free Black woman, Ellen Clark, and her four children as residents of the cove.

During the war, most people living in the cove maintained Union sympathies. Others, notably Foute, aligned themselves with the Confederacy. This division resulted in deep resentment between the sides.

Though several battles were fought in surrounding counties, Blount County was spared from the warring armies. However, people living in Cades Cove were not immune from the

Elijah Oliver cabin in Cades Cove, Tennessee, as it stood in 1975.

war's violence. Confederate guerrillas from North Carolina made frequent incursions. Raiders stole food from already lean pantries, as well as horses, livestock, and guns. Depredations continued even after East Tennessee was liberated by Federal troops in 1863.

Elijah Oliver—a man of 'Union principles' and the son of early cove settlers John and Lurena Oliver—moved his family up Rich Mountain for safety. But the war eventually found them. During one raid, Oliver was shot in the hand before surrendering and being held captive for two weeks. He escaped and returned to his overjoyed family.

Others were not so lucky. In 1864, Russell Gregory—a rancher, farmer, and the namesake of Gregory Bald—led a group of the local defense force in successfully defending the cove from a raid. Two weeks later, the guerrillas returned under cover of night and murdered Gregory in his bed.

With the return of peace, Oliver moved his family back to his farm in the cove, but the tranquil and neighborly atmosphere had changed. Acrimony settled like a pall over the area, compelling many families who had supported the Confederacy to leave the state entirely.

Daniel Foute was arrested by Federal authorities for his pro-Confederacy stance and died in a Knoxville jail.

Eking out a living in the cove was difficult at the best of times. During the war, shortages and raids made life far more precarious. But through defiance, courage, and determination, people like Elijah Oliver managed to survive until the war's end. The people of Cades Cove paid a price for their political loyalties, however. Neighbors turned against each other, many were victims of guerrilla violence, and in the end, Foute's vision of economic prosperity in the cove would not come to pass within his lifetime. ∽

Waynesville N C

March the 2 1866

I Alison Chandler

Dan this th 2 day of March bind my
self to work with Wesley Love ~~three~~ Four
months march Aprile May &
Jun for forty bushels of corn
one Pair of jains Pants & 2 shirts
one round about coat one Pair
Rhoes 2 Pairs socks Comencing
the second day of march 1866

Alison Ch [Seal]

Wesley Love [Seal]

Into the Unknown Sea of Freedom

1 8 6 6

Waynesville N.C.
March 2, 1866

I Alisson Chandler do this the 2 day of March bind my self
in work with Wesley Love four months March April May June
for forty bushels of corn one pair of jeans pants & 2 shirts
one round about coat one pair shoes 2 pairs socks Commencing
this the second day of March 1866

Alisson Chandler (seal)
Wesley Love (seal)

---

*Found between the pages of a Haywood County cobbler's ledger, this 1866 contract
between Alisson Chandler and Wesley Love, both newly emancipated, illustrates the
struggle that freed people faced to make a new life in an uncertain world.*

Africans were among the earliest non-native people in Southern Appalachia. Spanish explorers brought them to the area as enslaved participants of the expeditions. Later they lived with the Cherokee as both free and enslaved members of that society. In the antebellum era, African Americans settled the region of Western North Carolina as enslaved laborers and free Black people. But what happened after slavery was abolished following the Civil War?

Like other southern states, North Carolina was a political, social, and economic shambles after the Civil War. Emancipated Black people in Western North Carolina faced many of the same obstacles as their counterparts in other areas of the reunified South. Freedom from bondage left most ill-prepared and adrift in a landscape at once physically familiar and socially alien.

In the months after hostilities ceased, formerly enslaved African Americans found themselves unmoored in an area of economic devastation and upturned social order. They had their freedom, but little else. One thing they did have, though, was each other.

Found between the pages of a Haywood County cobbler's ledger, this 1866 contract between Alisson Chandler and Wesley Love, both newly emancipated, illustrates the struggle that freed people faced to make a new life in an uncertain world. According to the terms of the agreement, Chandler agreed to work for Love for four months in exchange for food and clothing—the barest necessities of life. This is a remarkable example of community building and mutual support in the face of government neglect and the indifference or hostility of the White majority.*

However, the federal government did extend a helping hand. To aid in the reconstruction of the war-torn South, the Bureau of Refugees, Freedmen, and

*After extensive research using census records and other primary and secondary sources, as well as consulting with local history experts, the author believes that this record represents a contract between two formerly enslaved people. Because they were considered property rather than human beings, they were not referred to by name in the 1850 and 1860 United States Federal Census Slave Schedules. This makes the task of tracing postwar family, where they lived, and their movement extremely difficult. In addition, enslaved people often took the last name of their enslavers, as their familial identity was sundered by the institution that stole them from their homes in Africa and transported them as human commodities to the Caribbean islands and North America. A lack of written records and reliable documentation makes researching the history of individual African Americans in the Reconstruction era extremely difficult.

Proclamation 95, the Emancipation Proclamation, was issued on January 1, 1863, by President Abraham Lincoln. The document changed the legal status of enslaved people living in states under rebellion as well as those living in areas occupied by Federal forces. It also reframed the war from merely a struggle to save the Union to a war to end slavery. Image courtesy of Library of Congress.

Abandoned Land, generally referred to as the Freedmen's Bureau, operated from 1865 to 1872. The bureau was responsible for managing all matters relating to freed people and refugees (both Black and White), as well as the redistribution of land seized or abandoned during the war.

The primary goal of the agency was to help formerly enslaved people to become self-sufficient. In some states, the organization successfully established schools, aided in the legalization of marriages performed during enslavement, and helped freed people to reunite with families or relocate to other parts of the country.

Unfortunately, the Freedmen's Bureau in North Carolina was severely understaffed and underfunded, increasing the likelihood that newly emancipated people would remain without housing and other necessities. An additional hurdle was the fact that the Haywood County branch was managed from the subdistrict office in Asheville.

To prevent widespread starvation in North Carolina in the immediate aftermath of the war, the bureau distributed more than 500,000 rations. The largest percentage went to the surviving families of Confederate soldiers who had died during the war. It has been estimated that, of the more than 300,000 formerly enslaved people in the state, only 5,000 received food aid from the bureau.

To make matters more complex, land was almost impossible to acquire. Some had been abandoned during the war for lack of labor, and the bureau saw fit to return much of it to ex-Confederates. Though the Freedmen's Bureau helped African Americans purchase land in some areas of the state in the first few months after the war, little or no land was available in Haywood County. Many Black farmers had little choice but to accept positions in sharecropping or tenant farming or were forced to leave the area entirely. Often, any farming done by the newly freed people was for their former enslavers. This situation created yet another system of labor that benefited the landowner to the detriment of the farmer, frequently resulting in another form of enslavement.

Unsurprisingly, many White people actively resisted the new order established by emancipation and supported the adoption of 'Black Codes'—laws designed to restrict the rights granted to formerly enslaved people. One restriction stated that any previously enslaved person wishing to enter into an apprenticeship had to offer their services to their former enslaver before anyone else. Though nominally in charge of their own labor, many were pressured back

TEACHING THE FREEDMEN.

Educating African Americans newly liberated from the shackles of slavery was one of the main objectives of the Freedmen's Bureau. Education was seen as key to equality and success during the Reconstruction era. Image courtesy of Tennessee State Library and Archives.

into servitude by the economic, legal, and political forces in action.

The fates of Alisson Chandler and Wesley Love remain obscured. Chandler is virtually invisible in the historic records, such as they are, and Love soon disappears. If Chandler moved to the western United States, emigrated to Liberia as part of the Back-to-Africa movement, or chose a new name and remained in Western North Carolina, we may never know. Love, along with his wife Willy and daughter Phebe, is last found in the 1870 federal census. Afterward, he too seems to vanish.

Despite stiff resistance from the White power structure and the federal government's failure to adequately protect these newly freed Americans, they managed to survive and thrive through sheer will and determination.

Since that time, African Americans have continued to shape the economy, culture, and history of Southern Appalachia. Though still largely invisible in the written history of the Smokies, they were—and are—integral to the region. Here we get an uncommon glimpse into the lives of two people navigating their way toward freedom through a troubled time in these mountains. ℰ∙ↄ

<u>he deer comes by the stand.</u>

By Charles Egbert Craddock

The woods are still, the winds scarce stir,
The drooping branches of the fir,
Whose shad'wing gloom is o'er me flung
Where lying low the roots among,
With watchful eye and ready hand,
I wait till the deer comes by the stand.

The pool reflects the silent sky,
The clouds in silent waters lie,
The noonday's sleep is on the birds,
The noonday's thirst is on the herds
Of red deer, hid on mountain's brink,
I wait until they come down to drink.

The noonday's languor stills my blood,
The noonday's sunshine pours its flood

40

Such a Charming Writer
Mary Noailles Murfree

1 8 7 8

———— *//* ————

Contemporary readers will be familiar with dramatic Southern Appalachian sagas like *Cold Mountain* by Charles Frazier and *Serena* by Ron Rash. These novels share the majestic Great Smoky Mountains as a backdrop and portray the lives of iconic mountaineers. Twentieth-century Appalachian literature is replete with masters such as Thomas Wolfe and James Dickey. But some contend that the person who put this region on the literary map was a woman from Tennessee named Mary Noailles Murfree.

Born in 1850 in Murfreesboro, Tennessee, the town named in honor of her grandfather, Murfree was the daughter of a prominent lawyer and a socialite mother. At four she contracted a fever that left her partially paralyzed for the rest of her life. Unable to participate in strenuous physical activity, she lived the life of the mind and became a voracious reader. Her father, an author himself, encouraged her to explore her literary and artistic passions.

After moving with her family to Nashville, Murfree attended the Nashville Female Academy. Upon graduation she moved to Philadelphia and enrolled in the Chegary Institute, a finishing school for young women. There she became fluent in French, Italian, and Latin and developed a deep love for

Writing under the male pseudonym Charles Egbert Craddock, Mary Noailles Murfree published dozens of short stories and novels depicting life in the American South.

Portrait of Mary Noailles Murfree who published under the name Charles Egbert Craddock.

music and poetry. She returned home after graduating in 1869 and read law under her father's tutelage for a time, though she never practiced.

She began writing in 1874 under the male pseudonym Charles Egbert Craddock. Male authors dominated the mid-19th-century literary world, while female writers faced an uphill battle for acceptance and success. In 1855, Nathaniel Hawthorne complained to his publisher that "America is now wholly given over to a damned mob of scribbling women." Though Hawthorne would later regret his "vituperation on female authors," his comment underscored a real bias that forced many to mask their gender. Murfree used her pen name throughout her career, even after revealing her true identity in 1885 to Thomas Bailey Aldrich, editor of the *Atlantic Monthly.*

Murfree published dozens of short stories and novels depicting life in the American South. In 1878, the *Atlantic Monthly* published her first short story, "The Dancin' Party at Harrison Creek," which was set in Southern Appalachia. She wrote in a genre known as American literary regionalism, or 'local color,'

MARTIN B. STONE, FUNDO "SANTA ANA", PITRUFQUEN.— (Chile)

NO RESPONDO POR NINGUNA MERCADERÍA REMITIDA POR F. C. DEL E. POR MI CUENTA, SI NO ESTÁ ASEGURADA

SU VALOR ÍNTEGRO INCLUIDO VALOR FLETE F. C.

Pitrufquén. Chile.   December 25th 1921.

Post Master.   Murfreesboro. Tennessee. U S.

My Dear Sir.

        Please to excuse the liberty of an old man,and kindly
tell me,if you know,if Miss M E Murfree, more widely known as
Charles Egbert Craddock(Nome de Plume) is still alive. If I am not
mistaken,she is a native of your city,and I believe that she married
many years since. Her first novel,issued along in 1885 or 86,had a
very widespread and highly merited circulation,and caused quite a stir
in literary cicles,and at the same time much guessing as to who the
author really was,her disguise completely misleading the whole public,
even her father and others of her family and friends,had not the least
inkling that it was written by she. I read it while in California,I
believe in 1886,and have read others of her most delightfull stories,
but not all,as I came here to Chile in the month of February of 1890.
I have always tried to keep note of her doings,as she was such a charming writer,and I being a Kentuckian,(Harrodburg,Mercer Co) and only
a short distance from where she was born,and where the scenes of her
stories were layed (or laid ?),although the Great Smoky Mts are quite
a distance from your city,and it has been so many years reading of them
she was born,that I may be mistaken,in thinking it happened in you city.
But in any case,you,as a fellow countryman of hers,will undoubtly know
and can easily set me at right,and at the same time any news regarding
herself and her literary labors will be most sincerely recieved and
apreciated,as if she was an old friend,as I have passed so many idle
hours,delighted and intensely intertained by her graphic pen,with the
use of words that had otherwise faded from my memory,words only used
there in Tenn and in Ky. Thanking you before hand, I am yours most
truly.   *Martin B. Stone*
P. S. Her first novel,if I am not mistaken,was "Wher the Battle was
Fought.

This letter written by a native Kentuckian living in Chile was addressed to the postmaster of Murfreesboro, Tennessee, the hometown of Mary Noailles Murfree. Martin B. Stone was a long-time fan of Murfree, whom he characterized as "such a charming writer." This is an example of the many letters she received during her life.

Fort Scott. Kas
July 22nd 85

Miss Murfree

My dear Young Lady
You must pardon
this intrusion, but I cannot
resist the impulse to write
& express my feeling of
admiration for you, after
reading the Aug no - of
the "Atlantic" with your
your serial. I never have
been so charmed in my
life in any work - your
Pen Pictures are so life
like - "Pete Cayce" & "Amos
Teemes Mollins" & the
chicken in the door, are
so clear, I wish I were
an artist, I could

Fort Scott, Kas
July 22nd 85

Miss Murfree

   My dear young Lady you must pardon this intrusion, but I
cannot resist the impulse to write & express my feeling of
admiration for you, after reading the Aug no_of the "Atlantic" with your serial. I never have been so charmed in my
life in any work-your pen pictures are so life like-"Pete
Cayce" & "Amos Jeemes mother" & the chicken in the door, are
so clear, I wish I were an artist, I could

In this letter, Jennie Haynes, a fan from Fort Scott, Kansas, makes observations about characters in The Prophet of the Great Smoky Mountains *as if she knows them person-ally, a testament to the Murfree's ability to connect with her readers.*

paint them- & the Mountains & ravines with light & shadow, are so beautifully portrayed by your wonderful pen. We have been reading the work aloud in a library circle of which I am the Pres. & my enthusiasm has caused many other to obtain it also. I alone in the club, felt that "Dorindy" was in love with the "Prophet"-several of the club, felt it was Amose James, & one a naval officer's wife felt that she was no vascillating girl-& that she was in love with- "Rick" but I must not weary you with our speculations. I must however express my gratitude to you for the restoration of the Prophets faith. I almost cried when he made his confession, & feared that he would fall back still lower, but Oh! Miss Murfree, his confession of Savior, & his sacrifice in defence of his Lord, in expiation of his sin, is such a powerful ending, & such a unanswerable argument "that the he can't argyfy the subject, he ____ there is a savior."

I used to admire Mrs. Bennett, but will never read another of her works after "Fro one administration" & Miss Woolson in "Anne" also lowered the standard of morals-but your work is so pure & lofty.

I hope you will pardon me, & if so will
signify by sending me your autograph,
to add to a very valuable collection
which I have of portraits & autographs
combined-in a large picture 60 by 40
in.-& which I propose sending to next
Exposition, & which will be so incom-
plete without your valued signature.
I remain sincerely your admirer

Jennie Hoyle Haynes
To Chas E Craddock

and was one of its early architects. This style of writing emphasized the dialects, customs, and history of a particular region. Where Missouri had Mark Twain, and Georgia had Joel Chandler Harris, East Tennessee had Murfree. Though the style fell out of favor early in the 20th century, it was extremely popular in its day, and Murfree is still considered one of its best exemplars.

The Prophet of the Great Smoky Mountains and *In the Tennessee Mountains*, both published in 1885, were the first works of fiction to bring popular attention to Tennessee and the Smokies. According to a 1914 review in the *Commercial Appeal*, "She has made friends with the Tennessee mountains. She has taken them into her confidence, and they have yielded her the secret of their allurement."

In 1885, the president of a Fort Scott, Kansas, book club wrote to Murfree gushing about how much her group loved reading *The Prophet of the Great Smoky Mountains*: "I never had been so charmed in my life in any work—your pen pictures are so lifelike." Someone from Pitrufquén, Chile, wrote the postmaster of Murfreesboro in 1921 asking after Murfree, saying, "I have always tried to keep note of her doings, as she was such a charming writer." Murfree was so well thought of that there was a well-organized but unsuccessful movement to name a peak in the newly formed national park after her pen name, Craddock.

She would face derision later, as would most local-color authors, from critics who characterized this genre as unflattering and offensive. Passages like "'Waal,' said Amos at last, rising, 'I'd better be a-goin'. 'Pears like ez I hev wore out my welcome hyar,'" were highlighted to denigrate this literary style and its writers.

As a child, Murfree spent many summers at the family's cottage in the Cumberland Mountains spa town of Beersheba Springs, Tennessee. Later, she often vacationed at Montvale Springs near Maryville, Tennessee. Some say these experiences acquainted her with the folkways of Southern Appalachian mountain communities. That's unlikely given her family's status and the affluent resort-like atmosphere of both places.

When the local color genre fell out of favor, Murfree attempted to change with the literary times, publishing several books in the newly popular historical romance style. Though well received, they failed to match her earlier successes. Her last published work, *The Story of Duciehurst: A Tale of the Mississippi*, was released in 1914. She died in 1922.

Murfree, and other authors like her, brought national attention to Appalachia. Though her writing perpetuated some of the negative stereotypes surrounding the mountaineer, it also paved the way for later female Appalachian authors like Wilma Dykeman and Nikki Giovanni. ♥

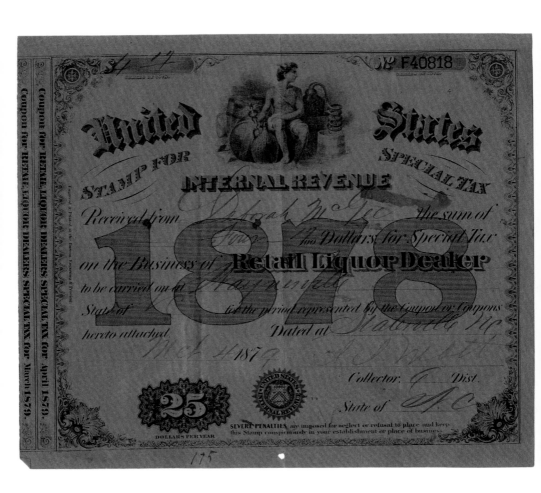

No. F40818

United States

STAMP FOR
SPECIAL TAX

INTERNAL REVENUE

Received from *Deborah McGee* the sum of *four* Dollars for Special Tax

on the Business of **Retail Liquor Dealer**

to be carried on at *Asheville*

State of for the period represented by the coupon or coupons

hereto attached. Dated at *Statesville N.C.*

Mch 4 1879

25
DOLLARS PER YEAR

Collector, *9* Dist.

State of *N.C.*

SEVERE PENALTIES are imposed for neglect or refusal to place and keep
this Stamp conspicuously in your establishment or place of business

175

Accounting for a Life

1 7 8 5

Concealed in the pages of a 19th-century store ledger is the tale of a mountain woman and the remarkable life she made. Through this document we discover the fascinating story of Deborah McGee of Waynesville, North Carolina, who seized important moments to create opportunities for herself and her community.

McGee, whose previous name was Milliken, was born in Tennessee around 1810. By the 1830s, she owned roughly 100 acres of land in Cocke County, Tennessee, and in 1841 received a 25-acre grant from the state in her own name. That was a noteworthy achievement. Though single White women could own land—and indeed had more legal protections than if married—land ownership among women in Southern Appalachia was uncommon.

Sometime between 1840 and 1850, Deborah Milliken left Tennessee and married John McGee of Waynesville, North Carolina. She brought along her younger sister, Elizabeth, who was "crippled for life," according to the 1860 census. Deborah settled into the life of a farm wife until her husband's death in 1856.

Naming her executor of his will, John had left to her "the town lot upon which I now live, all the notes and accounts I may have on hand, and a cow." At a crossroads, McGee chose an unexpected path. Rather than farm

Deborah McGee of Waynesville, North Carolina, was licensed by the Internal Revenue Service to retail liquor and collect taxes on the sales, as evidenced by this special tax license issued to her in 1879. This kept her on the legal side of the alcohol trade.

875 | 885

Black Berry Wine Aug[...]

[...] of well picked black b[...]
[...] of water let them sta[...]
[...] this time the scum mu[...]
[...] Liquer then strained [...]
[...]ut 3 pounds of suga[...]
[...] Liquer into a vesse[...]
[...] + gain for two or [...]
[...] way and in t[...]
[...] it off and to e[...]
[...] full of frenc[...]
[...]e Deborah M[...]

on her own, the 47-year-old mountain woman became an entrepreneur. By 1860, she had established herself as a relatively successful merchant, her new occupation being "retailer of spirits."

From about 1860 to 1880, McGee owned and operated an inn or tavern in Waynesville. Its ledger, covering the years 1865 to 1880, details a successful business. She rented rooms to the highland drovers, who drove cattle and hogs to market, and drummers, the salespeople who 'drummed up' sales from town to town. McGee also sold commodities like eggs, bacon, tobacco, and liquor by the glass or bottle. It's apparent from the ledger entries that her trade in alcohol was brisk and profitable.

Whiskey was a major commodity across the 19th-century American South and an economic opportunity for farmers. In the mountains of Southern Appalachia before the coming of the railroad, where access to adequate roads was a problem, farmers had a choice. They could take smaller crops of corn to market, or they could distill their corn into whiskey.

Distilling the corn meant larger profits. Some distillers sold the whiskey themselves. Others sold to people like Deborah McGee, who in turn sold liquor by the drink or by the bottle. Countless entries in the ledger show the purchase of liquor from local distillers, as well as the purchase of fermentable products such as corn and fruit. It's likely that, if McGee wasn't distilling whiskey and fruit brandy herself, she was providing the necessary ingredients for those who did.

But McGee was no bootlegger. She was licensed by the Internal Revenue Service to retail liquor and collect taxes on the sales, as evidenced by this special tax license issued to her in 1879. This kept her on the legal side of the alcohol trade. Over the years, the city of Waynesville issued dozens of permits approving the retail sale of "spiritous

This fragment of a recipe for blackberry wine was found inside the ledger Deborah McGee used to record her business transactions. McGee made wine, brandy, and other alcoholic beverages with fruit purchased from local famers. McGee was licensed to sell the intoxicating drinks she distilled and fermented.

liquor," undoubtedly to McGee as well.

The end of the Civil War brought many changes, and McGee's place in the community positioned her to take advantage of another opportunity. In 1866, she was appointed United States postmaster for Waynesville and served until at least 1869.

This wasn't unheard of, as rising numbers of women served as postmasters after the war. Since applicants had to swear that they had not voluntarily served the Confederacy or as soldiers in the Confederate military, many men were barred from this important role—paving a new path for women. By the mid-1890s, there were over 6,000 female postmasters managing more than 10 percent of all post offices.

McGee's next accomplishment, though, was decidedly unique. In 1869, she was one of only 1,100 people in North Carolina licensed by the federal government to retail liquor. And according to the 1870 Population Schedule of the Census, there were only two women in North Carolina listed as "traders in liquor and wine," making her an extreme rarity. By 1880, that number had increased to three, though she died before she could be included in the count.

McGee died in May 1880. We know this because, written in the store's ledger, in a hand other than her own,

are the words: "Mrs. Deborah McGee died at Waynesville NC about half past 12 o'clock A.M. May 17th, 1880."

Deborah McGee made space for herself in arenas often dominated by men. She capitalized on the political and economic climate to provide for herself, her family, and her community. The business she built provided an outlet for local goods at a time when access to large markets was restricted by lack of reliable roads and transportation. Her business, and others like it, no doubt helped isolated mountain communities like Waynesville survive the harsh economic realities of mountain life for southern highlanders. ✌

1877

Meals give a way

Jan 1 8 2 6 3 1 5 5 3 6 1 8 4   23
      9 3 10 2   12 5 13 5 15 6   21
      17 2 18 11 19 4 20 1 22 5 23 4 24 5   22
      25 0 26 0 27 28 6 29 1

Mrs. Deborah McGee Died at Waynesville N.C. about half Past 12 O'clock A.M. May 17th 1880

This disconsolate entry in McGee's ledger records the cold facts of her death: "Mrs. Deborah McGee died at Waynesville NC about half past 12 O'clock A.M. May 17th 1880."

Pre-Park 20th-Century Writings and Documents

1924 – 1930

Letter written to W. W. Stanley
on Mt. Le Conte - at midnight -
January 31, 1927

Dear, dearer, dearest Alkali Ike,   *W. W. Stanley*
Which of us three do you most like?   *U.T. Entomologist*
    By the fire
    'Way up higher -
We're up here! - We aint no liar!

There was a young man from Cornell   *Dr. L. R. Hesler*
The names of most plants he could tell
    His first name was Lex,
    Hunted spores with his specks,
And now he is in Huggin's Hell.

There was a bug man named Cy   *(Crosby)*   *Cy Crosby*
On the mountains he always was spry,   *Cornell "spider"*
    He hunted a spider   *expert*
    But drank too much cider
And now we fear he will die.

There was a young girl named Willie   *Willa Love Galyon*
To her suitors she was always chilly, *then a* *U.T. Botany major*
    But when she gets warm
    She says, "there's no harm -
To give you a <u>kiss</u> is not silly!"

There was a nice man named Campbell   *Carlos C. Campbell*
Up the mountain trails he would scramble
    Nothing more would he want
    Than a trip up Le Conte.
Oh Lord! How that bird does ramble!

There is a Magician named Gluesing   *Mr. (Dr.) Gluesing*
Who's so slick 'twould appear he'd been greasing, *was a General*
    With cards and a thimble   *Electric scientist, -- who*
    He really was quite nimble *was a talented magician*
His friends he always was fleecing.

A fellow from Ohio named Camp   *"Red" Camp*
Hair as red as the light of a lamp   *Ohio State University,*
    As quick as a flash   *botanist*
    With his little mustache
The flappers in his class he would vamp.

Barber is the name of a man who is tall,   *Chas. I. Barber*
Among architects he is best of them all,   *Architect*
    Buildings he would design
    For the University - so fine
We know that they never will fall.

A Blizzard of Limericks

1924

The Great Smoky Mountains have long been a destination for outdoor enthusiasts, especially from the Knoxville area. Even before the park's establishment, hikers and campers flocked to the region for its rugged beauty. In 1924, a group of intrepid hikers, including several named in this letter, made a trip up Mount Le Conte that would impact recreation in the mountains to this day.

In the fall of 1924, Knoxvillians Carlos Campbell, Jim Thompson, Charles Barber, and several others spent an idyllic afternoon exploring Mount Le Conte, Chimney Tops, and Myrtle Point. Campbell described finding Myrtle Point so densely carpeted that they were able to remove their shoes and walk on mountain myrtle so deep their feet never touched the ground.

The trip had such an impact on the group that they formed the Smoky Mountain Hiking Club, with the express intent of introducing locals and visitors to the beauty and grandeur of the Great Smoky Mountains. The club would become one of the most ardent local voices for the preservation of the mountains as a national park, with many of its members playing roles of national importance.

The hiking club joined the newly formed Appalachian Trail Conference in 1925 and took over responsibility for the Smokies section of the national trail. They selected the route, marked

---

This letter, in the form of limericks, mentions several key figures in the local effort to build Great Smoky Mountains National Park. It was written after a near-disastrous night spent at LeConte Lodge.

Among our hikers
There are no pikers
        From Montana -- so far as I know
But he is speedy
For food he is greedy
        "Praise God from whom all blessings flow".

The Late Dr. H. M. Jennison
U.T. Botanist

There was a young girl named Evelyn
Whom the boys were always devilin',
        She was fat
        And her feet were flat
But it didn't keep her from revelin'.

Miss Evelyn Wells
U.T. Botany major

There was a young prof from Leeds
Who got in on all the feeds.
        At night after dark
        He sings like a lark
And is noted for chivalrous deeds.

?

Now here is our president Jim
Surely you ought to know him
        Lots of money he makes
        On the pictures he takes
Sittin' way out on a limb.

Jas. E. Thompson

There was a tow head named Bess
Who had sins to confess
        So she went to the church
        Person left her in the lurch
And now the whole things is a mess.

Miss Bess Avery
U.T. Botany major

There was a young man named Brock
Who married to get a good clock*
        But it wasn't no fun
        'Cause the thing wouldn't run,
So he put it in a Yiddisher's hock.

Brockway Crouch
Florist & Hiking
Club president

* The Hiking Club gave him & Elsie a
clock as a wedding present

60

The morning after the blizzard, January 1, 1928. Four unidentified survivors of the night Campbell memorialized in verse.

the trail, and were early advocates of overnight shelters along the AT, helping to build the first few in the 1930s.

The group also served as an adjunct to the Knoxville Chamber of Commerce. To promote the region as a tourist destination, club members often personally escorted important visitors into the mountains.

On December 31, 1927, a group of scientists visiting Nashville for a meeting of the American Association for the Advancement of Science traveled to Gatlinburg to climb Mount Le Conte at the invitation of the chamber. The group was guided by Campbell, Thompson, Barber, Harry Jennison, Brockway Crouch, and other members of the Smoky Mountain Hiking Club. The day began with mild weather in the 40s, but by the time they reached the summit, a blizzard had commenced, and the temperature dropped to zero.

In 1927, the only accommodation on the mountain was a dirt-floored cabin with bunks at one end and a fireplace at the other. Under milder conditions, this would have been adequate shelter, but the temperature was so low that the heat from the roaring fire barely radiated into the room. The cabin was so cold in fact that a bucket of water a few feet from the fire froze solid.

Sleep was impossible, so the scientists and their hiking club escorts spent the night crowded around the fire. They sang songs, swapped stories, and composed limericks about each other, forever immortalized in this letter from Campbell.

The party emerged from the shelter the next morning to find the blizzard had passed, leaving in its wake a 20-below-zero landscape of snow and ice. They survived their polar night and returned to Knoxville the following day.

ↄ ↄ ↄ

Hiking club members—from many stations of society and representing a variety of interests—were united by their passion for conservation. While all of the members supported the establishment of the national park, a handful played key roles.

Some, like Harry Jennison, were professional naturalists. Jennison was a professor of botany at the University of Tennessee from 1924 until his death in 1940. He was also a field agent for the US Department of Agriculture and spent many summers as an NPS wildlife technician. He built a massive herbarium of samples taken in the Smokies and was responsible for identifying plant species in the park, including a previously unknown variety of azalea on Clingmans Dome.

Another member was Brockway Crouch, a Knoxville florist and botanist, who often made forays into the mountains for materials to use in his arrangements. He published many articles about hikes in the Smokies and served on the Tennessee Nomenclature Committee, the group that helped finalize the names of many peaks, valleys, and waterways on the Tennessee side of the park.

Some members' efforts to build the park were more literal than others. Charles Barber was a prominent Knoxville architect who designed grand homes, churches, and commercial buildings. His contribution can be found in the design and construction of the park headquarters building in Gatlinburg, Tennessee.

The mountains have always inspired photographers, and club member Jim Thompson was no exception. A commercial photographer from Knoxville, he played a crucial role in communicating the beauty of the Smokies to people outside the region. Thompson's stunning photographs of peaks and vistas traveled around the country as part of presentations to elected officials, community groups, and other organizations with a vested interest in the establishment of a national park in the Southeast.

Perhaps the member most intricately tied to the creation of the park was Carlos Campbell. He used his position as manager of the Knoxville Chamber of Commerce to help advocate for the preservation of the mountains. As secretary of the Great Smoky Mountains Conservation Association (GSMCA), Campbell had a front-row seat for the drama that unfolded around the campaign to build a park. Later, he would use his position on the GSMCA board to guide park management during the first 30 years of its history.

The club's work was not finished once the park was established. Campbell and others would continue to fight to protect the park and hold accountable those who managed it for the public.

The Smoky Mountain Hiking Club still operates today. Though focused on promoting hiking in the park, it has expanded its outreach to include outdoor education and conservation awareness and continues to be an important advocate for the park. ℰℑ

It was in July 1923,
We were returning from a western business trip, & had just visited the Yellow Stone National Park.
I remarked that I thought the Great Smokies were as beautiful as any mountains we had seen in the West & I thought that with so many parks in the West there should be at least one in the East —
Mr. Davis agreed ~~and said~~ at once ^& said^ that he would see what he could do about it.
Upon his first business trip to Washington D.C. which he took frequently he called upon
Sec. Hubert Work, ^U.S. Dept of the Interior^ and told him what was in his mind & tried to paint for him the beauties of the Great Smokies —
(Robert Sterling Yard)

TENNESSEE

State Legislature
1925

Anne Davis,
For the Park and the People

1 9 2 5

The story of Anne Davis' role in helping to establish Great Smoky Mountains National Park appears simple on the surface, but the reality is more complex. Her handwritten note describes its beginning: "It was in July 1923, and we were returning from a western business trip and had just visited Yellowstone National Park. I remarked that I thought the Great Smokies were as beautiful as any mountains we had seen in the west and I thought that with so many parks in the west there should be one in the east."

Her husband Willis agreed, and on returning to Knoxville, Tennessee, began to garner support from both the local business community and his contacts in Washington.

Anne and Willis Davis were natives of Louisville, Kentucky, who moved to Knoxville in 1915 when Willis took over management of the Knoxville Iron Company. Willis was an influential local businessman and civic leader, belonging to the Knoxville Chamber of Commerce and the Knoxville Automobile Club, and was well-connected in Washington. Anne was equally civic-minded, being an early member of the Knoxville League of Women Voters and the Knoxville Garden Club.

In 1925, Anne Davis was elected to office, defeating nine male candidates. She was the first woman sent to state legislature from Knox County and only the third in the entire state to serve since the ratification of the 19th Amendment in 1920.

Gov. Austin Peay signed the legislation authorizing the purchase of Little River Company land. Left to right: Jeff Hunt, acting secretary to the governor; Speaker of the Senate Judge L. D. Hill; Representative Anne Davis; Gov. Peay; Mary Virginia Cox of the governor's office; Representative W. B. Hatcher; and Speaker of the House W. F. Barry, Jr.

They were a power team and, together, advanced the park's cause at the local, state, and national level.

In 1924, Davis announced her intention to run for the state legislature in order to support the effort to establish a national park in Southern Appalachia. In 1925, she was elected to office, defeating nine male candidates. Davis was the first woman sent to the legislature from Knox County and only the third in the entire state to

serve since the ratification of the 19th Amendment in 1920.

Davis rode a wave of progressive change into office, and once there she threw her support behind Governor Austin Peay, who had made the establishment of a national park in the Smokies one of his campaign promises for his 1923 election. Davis sponsored the legislation that would purchase more than 78,000 acres of land from the Little River Lumber Company—the kernel that would eventually become the park.

Garnering support for the bill was an uphill struggle. Representatives from western and middle Tennessee were reluctant to spend money on land in the eastern end of the state. In addition, the timber industry was lobbying hard for a national forest instead of a park. Davis worked closely with Peay to find a solution to the impasse.

She convinced the legislature to go into recess so that a fact-finding trip could be made to the mountains—a key event that solidified support for the bill. None of the legislators who attended the trip had been to the Smokies before, and they were "amazed to find these wonderful mountains" in their state.

Knoxville mayor Ben Morton convinced the city council to pay one third of the purchase price of the Little River Lumber Company land, an unheard-of contribution by a municipal entity. It was the deciding factor in gaining the support of western and middle

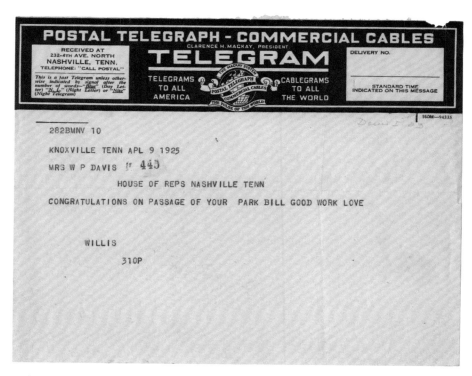

Telegram from Willis P. Davis to his wife, Anne, congratulating her on the passage of the legislation she introduced.

Tennessee lawmakers and ensured the legislation's passage.

Anne Davis' primary motivation in running for the state legislature may have been to help establish the park, but she also supported bills that benefited underserved members of the population, primarily women and children. While in office, Davis approved the formation of a domestic relations court in Knox County and reformed juvenile court laws. She introduced a bill for women to serve on grand juries and petit juries. She worked on legislation establishing the right of women to serve on county school boards and as factory inspectors—and granting married women property rights equal to those of single women.

Her work in the senate uplifted her constituency and helped establish the most visited national park in the United States. After leaving office, she was elected president of the Knoxville chapter of the League of Women Voters and, through that position, proposed legislation that built on her work in the senate. Her impact endures.

For years, Davis' contributions to the formation of the park were overshadowed by those of her husband and other prominent men in the movement. A ridge in the park is named in her honor, but some feel that commemoration through a minor geographic feature undervalues her considerable achievement.

One person who fully appreciated her effort at the time, though, was Governor Peay. Not only did he invite Davis to attend the signing of the legislation that approved the purchase of Little River Lumber Company land, the governor also presented her with the ostrich-quill pen he used to sign the bill. ✑

Personal

A. A. FELDING COMPANY
REAL ESTATE AND LOANS
108 EAST VINE AVENUE
KNOXVILLE, TENNESSEE

Mr Trimm
Altoss country
Col W. E. Chapman
City.

March 30-26.

Dear Col.

I am very much interested in the Smoky Mt project. it will be a knockout blow to the city to lose this chance. please have me mailed a list of Subscriptions turned in by the colored people through various Solicitors. names and amts agreed on. say nothing until you hear from me again which I expect will be by return after looking over such list. then you can let the press have same with proper story.

With my Best wishes
I Remain, Sincerely
Your friend
A. A. Felding

A Troubled Compromise

1 9 2 6

In the American South of the 1920s, there were few safe spaces for African Americans to experience the great outdoors recreationally. Known as the Jim Crow era, this period from the 1870s to the 1960s was characterized by a series of laws and social constraints designed to create a racial caste system.

Found primarily, though not exclusively, in the South, these state and local laws perpetuated the notion that Black people were second-class citizens and therefore undeserving of the same level of access and privilege granted to White people. As federally managed public lands, national parks offered the hope of democratized access to outdoor recreation, but there was little agreement about how to make this a reality on a state-by-state basis.

At the time, public spaces—including libraries, municipal parks, and public transportation—were segregated. Areas dedicated to outdoor pursuits were a relatively new feature in many states.

North Carolina's first state park opened in 1916. The Tennessee state park system wasn't established until 1929, with the opening of Nathan Bedford Forrest State Park. That park was named in honor of the Confederate

---

A. A. Fielding, a prominent African American realtor and political leader, was the son of one of the first Black physicians to open a practice in Knoxville after the Civil War. In this 1926 letter to David Chapman, then director of the Great Smoky Mountains Conservation Association Fielding asks for a list of "subscriptions turned in by the colored people."

A. A. FELDING COMPANY
REAL ESTATE AND LOANS
108 EAST VINE AVENUE
KNOXVILLE, TENNESSEE

March 31 - 26.

Col D C. Chapman
City.

Dear Col,

On Behalf of my people, in order to about double the amount raised by them by subscription for the Great Smoky Mountains National Park fund. I Hereby subscribe Three Hundred Dollars for said fund. With Our Very Best wishes that the Proposition will go over with out further delay.

We Remain
Respty yours
Mr & Mrs A. A. Felding

Civil War general and first Grand Wizard of the White supremacist hate group the Ku Klux Klan. Parks in both states were solely for White people until the establishment of segregated parks in the 1930s.

As this 1926 letter from A. A. Fielding illustrates, there was enthusiastic support among Knoxville's Black community for the establishment of Great Smoky Mountains National Park. Fielding, a prominent African American realtor, was the son of A. A. Fielding Sr., one of the first Black physicians to open a practice in Knoxville after the Civil War. In this letter to David Chapman, then director of the Great Smoky Mountains Conservation Association, Fielding asks for a list of "subscriptions turned in by the colored people." A note written on the letter by Chapman to his secretary instructs her to supply Fielding with a record of these financial pledges.

The following day, Fielding responded to the report with a matching pledge to the park: "On behalf of my people, in order to about double the amount raised by them . . . I hereby subscribe three hundred dollars for said fund." Fielding's large matching contribution indicates that Knoxville's Black community pledged roughly the same amount. Adjusted for inflation, that would be more than $8,000 in 2023.

౭ ౭ ౭

In the pre-war era, many viewed the formation of a national park in the South as an opportunity to counter the effects of racial segregation. Though enshrined in law in southern states, segregation was less prevalent at the federal level, notable exceptions being the military and the District of Columbia. But when it was revealed that Shenandoah National Park, near Washington, DC, would build segregated facilities, Walter White, secretary of the NAACP, was dismayed.

Writing to Secretary of the Interior Harold Ickes in 1937, White asked if it was true that six recreation areas for White people and one for Black people were going to be established at

National Association for the Advancement of Colored People (NAACP) Chairman, Walter Francis White. Image courtesy of Smithsonian Institute.

Shenandoah. The NAACP viewed this as "the establishment of a Jim-crow project on federal territory" and went on record saying that it was "vigorously protesting against the inauguration of such a policy."

Ickes responded that it was the long-standing policy of the park service to "conform generally to the state customs with regard to accommodation of visitors." Most western national parks had been formed from existing federal lands. Southern parks differed significantly. These parks were composed of land purchased from individuals and businesses in cooperation with the states. As a result, the states expected that local regulations and laws would be applied inside national park boundaries, including Jim Crow laws.

The National Park Service was unwilling to alienate the southern states by openly ignoring local custom and law. When pressed by a visitor in 1936 about segregated facilities at Shenandoah, NPS Associate Director Arthur Demaray wrote, "Under no consideration does the National Park Service regard such separate facilities as any evidence of or intention towards race separation in the park." Demaray went on to say that there was nothing unusual about providing segregated amenities for "white and colored people to the extent only as is necessary to conform with the generally accepted customs long established in Virginia," and that the remainder of the park was not segregated.

❧ ❧ ❧

Charles Spurgeon Johnson, Fisk University. Image courtesy the Van Vechten Trust.

In 1937, Charles Johnson, then director of the Social Services Department at Fisk University, wrote to the director of the National Park Service, Arno B. Cammerer, questioning what the policy would be toward African Americans seeking recreation at Great Smoky Mountains National Park. Johnson wanted to know if it was the agency's duty to "insist upon the participation of all elements of the population" in the new park.

Cammerer admitted that was not the case. Though they had tried to be equitable in the way services were provided regardless of race, the park service had only planned minimal development for African Americans in the Smokies. Cammerer did promise that construction would follow demand.

The idea that facilities for Black visitors would only be built if the demand materialized was not reflected in GSMNP Superintendent Ross Eakin's master planning process. Planning documents from 1939 note, "There will be three Negro campgrounds shown on the Master Plan as follows at Mr. Eakin's request: Cades Cove; near Chestnut Branch and Fighting Creek Road: and opposite Collins Creek on the south side of the mountain near New Found Gap Highway."

Eakin believed that more amenities for the Black community would draw more Black visitors. In a 1941 memo to NPS Regional Director Thomas Allen, Eakin stated that "southern negroes will not utilize utilities unless they are designated for negroes."

Allen followed Cammerer's logic and argued that demand should dictate

Director of the National Park Service, Arno B. Cammerer. Image courtesy of Library of Congress.

need. Since African American visitation at the Smokies was minimal, there was no need to add separate facilities.

However, two segregated facilities were built in the Smokies. In 1939, comfort stations at Newfound Gap and Forney Ridge, both located near the state line between Tennessee and North Carolina, were constructed with segregated toilet facilities inside and a common entrance outside.

Meanwhile, in 1939, Interior Secretary Ickes had ordered that a large and convenient site at Shenandoah be "nonsegregated" and open to all users. Pinnacles Picnic Ground operated under this experimental guidance with no complaints, and by 1941, the policy had been extended to all the park's picnic grounds. By 1942, Ickes intended to extend this policy to all park service units in the South, but America's entry into war in 1942 put a hold on infra-structure development in all parks, including the Smokies.

Ultimately, the outbreak of World War II and growing changes in postwar America would end further debate regarding additional segregated facilities in southern national parks.

When construction of camp-grounds and picnic areas resumed in the Great Smoky Mountains after the end of the war, segregated facilities were not part of the plan. In 1948, President Harry Truman, after pressure from the NAACP, signed Executive Order 9981 effectively ending segregation within the US armed forces. And in 1950, vis-itor amenities at Shenandoah National Park were fully integrated.

In 1953, the segregated comfort stations in the Smokies were remodeled, and all evidence of official segregation in the park was removed. Decades later in 2010, the Forney Ridge comfort station was again remodeled—this time being transformed into a visitor contact station. Now the Clingmans Dome Visitor Contact Station, operated by Great Smoky Mountains Association, the location provides education and information to park visitors.

☙ ☙ ☙

During much of the 20th century, African American visitation to the Smokies was minimal. This belies the fact that the history of Black people in Southern Appalachia is vast and deep, though often overlooked. To illuminate the immense contributions of African Americans in this region, Great Smoky Mountains Association and Great Smoky Mountains National Park have embarked on the African American Experiences in the Smokes Project to share important but neglected stories with park visitors and the world. ☙

March 12, 1926.

Hon. Everett Sanders,
Secretary to the President,
Washington, D. C.

My dear Sir:

As you know, the proposed Great Smoky
Mountains National Park is now attracting much
attention throughout the country. In consideration of the interest which has been shown by
President Coolidge in this noteworthy project, it
has occurred to members of the directorate of the
Great Smoky Mountains Conservation Association,
sponsor of the park movement in Tennessee, that it
would be fitting to give to President Coolidge a
splendid specimen of bobcat which has just been
captured in the area which will be eventually
covered by the Great Smoky Mountains National Park.

The cat, quite commonly referred to as
wildcat, the zoological name of which is Felis
Rufa, is at present confined in a steel cage. It
is one of the largest for its age ever captured in
the Great Smokies, is in splendid condition, and
would be a welcome adjunct to the Washington Zoological Park. It is not yet full grown.

As a tribute to the proposed park, the
habitat of the bobcat, the specimen which we would
like to present to President Coolidge has been named
Smoky Bob.

This cat is a native of Sevier County,
which at the last national election was the strongest
Republican County in the country. The eleventh civil
district in which is situated Gatlinburg at the foot
of Mount LeConte, acknowledged outstanding mountain
personality of the East, and the scenic marvel of
the proposed park, presented a unique election

Bob and Calvin's Big Adventure

1926

Over its long history, the White House has been home to more pets than people. 'First Pets' have ranged from the commonplace—like James Madison's parrot, Macaw, or the Obamas' Portuguese water dog, Bo—to the more exotic and downright dangerous. Theodore Roosevelt, for example, kept a lion, a hyena, and a zebra, among others, while John Quincy Adams kept an alligator given to him by the Marquis de Lafayette.

Republican president Calvin Coolidge, who served from 1923 to 1929, was probably the most prolific collector of animals. During his time in office, he had 28 pets, including a selection of dogs, cats, birds, and fish, along with more exotic animals. From foreign dignitaries and potentates, he received lion cubs, bears, a wallaby, and a pygmy hippo. Coolidge was even given a bobcat named Smoky Bob, a gift from Col. David Chapman and the Great Smoky Mountains Conservation Association.

To honor the president for his support and interest in the establishment of a national park in the Great Smoky Mountains, the board of directors of the conservation association thought

---

In a letter to Everett Sanders, secretary to the president, Chapman represented the bobcat as having "just been captured in the area which will be eventually covered by the Great Smoky Mountains National Park . . . and is one of the largest for its age ever captured." But in a letter to the director of the National Zoological Park, Dr. William Mann, Chapman confessed that the animal was captured as a kitten and had been "more or less domesticated."

record at that time when it returned 442 votes for President Coolidge, 11 for Mr. Davis, and none for Senator LaFollette. Smoky Bob was born and raised wi within a few miles of this spot.

Will you kindly let us know immediately if President Coolidge will accept this present? The bobcat will be shipped directly on receipt of acknowledgement of this letter.

Very sincerely yours,

David C. Chapman
Chairman of the Board.

DCC:lvm

Smoky Bob awaiting his trip to the White House, 1926.

it would be fitting to gift the president with an animal from Southern Appalachia. To make the gift even more attractive, Smoky Bob was said to have been captured in Sevier County, which, Chapman wrote, "at the last national election was the strongest Republican County in the country."

In a letter to Everett Sanders, secretary to the president, Chapman represented the bobcat (*Lynx rufus*) as having "just been captured in the area which will be eventually covered by the Great Smoky Mountains National Park . . . and is one of the largest for its age ever captured." But in a letter to the director of the National Zoological Park, Dr. William Mann, Chapman confessed that the animal was captured as a kitten and had been "more or less domesticated."

The Coolidges received pets as gifts from all over the world and never turned one away. A woman in

Mississippi sent a raccoon to the White House with instructions that it be fattened up and served at Thanksgiving. The First Lady declined to cook the animal and instead named it Rebecca and made her part of the household. Smoky Bob never actually became a household pet, however. Given the fact that many of the First Family's pets would have been viewed

Grace Coolidge and her pet raccoon, Rebecca. Image courtesy of Library of Congress.

as prey by Smoky Bob, that was probably a good thing. Instead, Bob's new home would be the National Zoo. As a matter of fact, most of the Coolidges' more exotic pets ended up residing there.

Bob arrived by train at his new home on March 20, 1926, and was transferred to a large outdoor enclosure complete with a label stating his name, home range, and status as a gift

to the president from the GSMCA. In May 1926, President Coolidge signed a bill passed by Congress that allowed for the establishment of Shenandoah National Park and Great Smoky Mountains National Park. While it is highly unlikely that the gift of a bobcat influenced the president's decision, Chapman no doubt saw a way to hedge his bet and provide the president with a unique addition to the White House menagerie. ✌

$80 A highest value in Cove

Highest ever paid 7 A for $100.00 per acre

John J. Verlund at $3000.00

$787.50 $900.00

70 acre

Cades Cove, Tenn.
June 18, 1928.

Mr. John D. Rockefeller Jr.
New York City, N.Y.

My Dear Mr Rockefeller:—

Relative to the Great Smoky Mountain National park and the Rockefeller donation,

I wish to call your attention to the following existing facts, viz:

Cades Cove is the most beautiful spot of all the world, six miles long and three miles wide, level as a floor and very futile, is inhabited by one hundred and ten families or a population of six hundred people. Has four Churches, three stores, and a number of Cemeteries. It is an old established Community

---

In this 1928 letter to philanthropist John D. Rockefeller Jr., Cades Cove resident Walter Gregory pleads for the protection of his community and way of life.

Help Us, Rockefeller, You're Our Only Hope!

1 9 2 8

The coming of the national park brought drastic change to the Great Smoky Mountains. Families that had lived in the area for more than one hundred years would be uprooted in the name of conservation and tourism.*

While residents of Cataloochee, Smokemont, Greenbrier, and the Sugarlands would soon be compelled to sell their land through the exercise of eminent domain, Cades Cove inhabitants expected to avoid the fate of those in neighboring communities. Unlike people in other areas of the park, those in the cove had reason to be hopeful that the final park boundary would exclude their little valley. They took to heart assurances from elected officials and park commission members that they wouldn't lose their homes. But a trust in words and good intentions lulled residents into a false sense of security.

Long before the establishment of the national park, the cove was

---

The history of forced displacement of people in the Smokies began long before the creation of the national park. The Cherokee people who have lived here for millennia were eventually forced off their ancestral homeland after years of duplicitous treatment by the colonial and later federal governments. This tragic saga culminated in the Indian Removal Act of 1830 and their subsequent violent removal to land in Oklahoma. On the route known as the Trail of Tears, thousands died of disease, starvation, and exposure before reaching their ultimate destination. Some Cherokee people, however, successfully resisted forced removal and managed to remain in the Smokies, while others returned to the area from Oklahoma. Known as the Eastern Band of Cherokee Indians, they live primarily in the Qualla Boundary in Western North Carolina.

having been settled over one hundred years ago.

Is very productive as a farming district. Its people are very prosperious. and happy and do not want to give up their homes for Park purposes.

At first the Park people did not want it and went to a great deal of trouble to assure the people they would not be disturbed or molested in the least, but after they secured the Rockefeller fund then they set about to take it.

Consequently our people our very much disturbed and distressed over the matter. Our land is valued very high from one hundred to three hundred per acre. and is absolutely not needed in the park.

noted for its wild game, abundant water, and fertile land. For hundreds of years, Cherokee people enjoyed the bounty found there. The first Europeans settled in the cove in the early 1820s and within a few decades had established a robust community. By the 1850s, the population of the valley surpassed 500, and a thriving economy developed complete with and, we have made many appeals to the park people, but to no avail, now we come to you with our troubles.

It was the Rockefeller money that made the park a reality, without it the park would have been a failure, we most respectfully ask, beg, and implore you to request the park people to leave us outside, the park area, or you will withdraw the Rockefeller donation.

Hundreds of Thousands of feet of Lumber are being cut each day by Lumberman inside the park area and, if the park area commission would devote their time to these most important details, it would be of much greater value to the park interests.

schools, churches, stores, mills, and a post office.

By the early 1920s, the cove appeared poised to benefit from the growth of motor tourism. The construction of a new road to Townsend in 1922 made access to the area much easier. Hoping to benefit from the close proximity of the proposed national park, John Oliver built a lodge to house

H.

GSMNCA.IX-9-d

I can get hundreds of people to certify to the facts I have just stated if desired.

Hoping and trusting you will give all this important matter your most thoughtful consideration, I am yours most Respectfully,

D. Walter Gregory,

Cades Cove,

Tenn.

John D. Rockefeller Jr., philanthropist, financier, and conservationist. Rockefeller helped establish Acadia, Shenandoah, Grand Teton, and Great Smoky Mountains National Park. Image courtesy of Library of Congress.

guests and began a guide service. A developer from Maryville purchased land on Cades Cove Mountain with an eye to building a vacation resort. Though never realized, the development—dubbed "Summer Haven"—was to be modeled after the resort community in Elkmont.

As late as 1928, rumors were circulating that the decision had been made to leave the cove outside the park boundary. David Chapman, chairman of the Great Smoky Mountains Conservation Association, wrote to Blount County Clerk George Roberts: "No definite decision has been made about Cades Cove. . . . One of the factors that will be given consideration is that they have run prices up very much higher than they were in the beginning and looks like it is higher than it ought to be."

The announcement in March 1928 that the Laura Spelman Rockefeller Foundation would donate $5 million toward the establishment of Great Smoky Mountains National Park brought the realization that cove residents might indeed lose their homes. In addition, a bill from the Tennessee General Assembly providing funds to purchase land and the legal right to exercise eminent domain shocked locals into action. Some, like John Oliver, would fight in the courts to protect their ability to stay on their land.

Others appealed to the humanity of John D. Rockefeller to intercede on their behalf. This letter written to Rockefeller by Walter Gregory in June 1928 made a passionate case for Rockefeller to act as the cove's savior. In plain, eloquent language, Gregory gives a brief history of European settlement in the cove, extolls the natural beauty of the area, and implores Rockefeller "to request to park people to leave us outside the park area or you will withdraw the Rockefeller donation." In the end, the die was cast—Cades Cove would be included within the boundary of the park.

Once in motion, the purchase of property moved rapidly. By the end of 1929, almost half the farms in the area had been purchased by the park commission. Many who sold didn't leave immediately but stayed in their homes, having negotiated lease agreements with the commission. But by 1936, most families had moved out, leaving only a dozen living on leases, the last of those being Kermit Caughron, who lived in Cades Cove until the late 1990s. ❧

Nov-24.38.
Kirksville. mo-

Miss Louisa walker and
sisters. Sevierville Rout.7.Tenn-
dear cousins as j am alone to
night & very lonesome j will try
to write u all a few lines in ans-
of yours j recieved some time
ago. like always j was glad to
hire from u glad u were all
well at that time. j am well at
presant only a little homesick to
se u all on thanksgiving and
have another big squirl dinner
like we had four years ago
today if u remember j come to
your house on thanksgiving
4. years ago today with some
squirls & u all cooked them &
we had squirl & dumplins the
last good mess of squirls j
ever had. j hope this finds u
all well & enjoying your selves.
j guess u had a big dinner
to day. how is every body in
general. how is jantes folks.
also carolines. does john shelton
stay at home now. does Hayel &
Effa work at Knoxville now. tell
Hayel when u se her j would
love to have a few lines from her.
what has become of Dan & Georgia
they never write any more.

Harp Singing and Squirrel Stew

1 9 3 0

———————

The Walker family lived in the Great Smoky Mountains for so long they were woven into the very fabric of the landscape. Arriving in the area after the American Revolution, they put down roots in the verdant hollows and coves on the Tennessee side of the Appalachian Mountains.

The most widely known member of this family, John N. Walker, returned from service in the Union army after the Civil War to make a home for himself and his wife, Margaret Jane, in Little Greenbrier.

Over the years, as the family grew, the farm grew too, eventually encompassing more than 122 acres. Though they had 11 children—seven girls and four boys—the family lived in a modest two-story log cabin, expanded slightly by the addition of a kitchen on the back and a porch on the front. There were also a barn, corn crib, blacksmith shop, pig pen, spring house, apple house, and tub mill. The cabin never had electricity, running water, or even an outhouse.

Not all Walkers stayed in the mountains. In the late 1880s, John's younger brother William moved with his wife, Sarah, and son, Bert, to Missouri. Though Bert was only in his 20s when his family left East Tennessee, his

---

In a series of letters written to his cousin Louisa Walker, Bert Walker mentioned living in a boarding house in Kirksville, Missouri, 40 miles north of his farm in Drake Township. Unable to find steady work, he spent time going to the movies, reminiscing about Tennessee, and writing his cousins, the Walker sisters, in the mountains.

well this has been a long & lonesome day. it seams like sunday here in town all the stores are closed to day. they are having a big dance at the Hall to night j' was up there awhile. dident se many people j' new & come back to my Roome. j' have bin disatisfied all day. j' went to a good show just after noon but dident enjoy it very well. j' havent had mutch work for three weeks & j' always get disatis= fied when j'me not working. well they are having some excitement just now j' here the fire alarm. j' can see the fire just about three or four Blocks from where j' am. well j' wish j' could step in to your dore to night & make u all a good visit. j' am like the song j' herd in the show to day. ever since j' starled to rome j'me not at home in this world any more.--- its a hard life.-- but it cant last always.-- j'me thinking of leaving here in the next few days if j' dont get started to work. j' dont no yet where j'le go to. it has been prety cold here for afew days. we had one little snow about 2. weeks ago. well j'le ring off & go to bed. wishing u all good luck. Bert—

P. S. am sending u some
pictures. thought u might
like to se what jive been
doing. i believe ime getting wilder
all the time. i feel as wild as a
wolf & as lonesome as an owl to
night. nearly as wild as i was
the day i ate dinner at your house
and will Lawson & mary & jim Law-
& john w— & Dan & Georgia & Pearl
and we all had an old harp singing
out on the poarch. man. man.
those are days that has gon by. and
will neverhapen so again. i guess
hetty has forgoten all about that
day.-- well it would be imposible
for that to all hapen again----
wishing u all the very best of luck
and sunshine & flowers all along
down the lane of life. hoping to
here from u all again Bert.-

P. S. am sending u all a feather
off of part of my thanksgiving
dinner.. a good dinner. Bert

Bert Walker, an unidentified member of this work crew, threshing wheat in Missouri, ca. 1920. Bert farmed for several decades with his family in the Drake Township until the economic pressures of the Great Depression forced him to find work elsewhere.

ties to the mountains and his cousins, the Walker sisters, remained strong. He still missed "home" when he wrote this letter in his 70s.

Bert's life in Missouri was less than idyllic. In 1899, his first wife, Sarah, died in childbirth along with their child. Walker remarried a few years later and had another child, Waney, with his second wife, Ada. The family farmed in Drake Township, Missouri, for several decades, but by the late 1930s, the hard times had found them. Waney died in 1937, and a poor economy forced Bert

to leave the farm to find work.

In a series of letters written to his cousin Louisa Walker, Bert mentioned living in a boarding house in Kirksville, Missouri, 40 miles north of his farm in Drake Township. Unable to find steady work, he spent time going to the movies, reminiscing about Tennessee, and writing his cousins, the Walker sisters, in the mountains.

After John Walker's death in 1921, the remaining five sisters—Margaret, Louisa, Hetty, Martha, and Polly—continued to live in the house alone.

Family members and friends helped with many of the daily farm chores. The sisters' farm was never abundantly productive, however. Even when their father was alive and their brothers lived at home, the farm had not produced a surplus. Still, they raised nearly everything they consumed, including the cotton and wool for their clothes and the leather for their shoes.

Life in Little Greenbrier was difficult and often arduous, but it was not without great beauty. In addition to most of their food, the sisters grew more than 100 varieties of flowers and other ornamental plants. Louisa was a poet and artist. Friends and family gathered in the home for evenings of music and song. Bert Walker fondly recalled sessions of 'shape note' singing, a tradition

The Walker sisters, from left to right Hettie, Louisa, Martha, Polly, and Margaret, 1938.

in Southern Appalachia in which the shape of particular notes determines how the melody is sung.

The sisters worked hard to provide for their daily needs and to make sure enough was 'put by' for the winter. They preserved things like corn, cabbage, peas, beans, potatoes, apples, and meat.

Meals were often bountiful—especially those shared with friends and family—and prepared from foods grown on their farm as well as foraged from the surrounding mountains. Particularly meaningful to Bert Walker was squirrel stew and dumplings, a meal he remembered enjoying the last time he had visited the sisters, having provided the squirrel himself.

Change would also visit the Walker sisters' home in Little Greenbrier. The establishment of Great Smoky Mountains National Park in 1934 brought disruption to everyone who lived in the mountains, as hundreds of families were forced to sell their land and move.

The sisters, however, were granted a reprieve. Ross Eakin, superintendent of the newly established national park, was concerned that a court case forcing the sisters to sell their land would result in adverse publicity and possibly a large settlement. Instead, they were offered a lifetime lease, allowing them to stay on their land.

The Walker sisters became as popular a tourist attraction as the scenic mountains themselves. People flocked to Little Greenbrier to see a romanticized interpretation of how life was lived more than 100 years before. The sisters capitalized on this by selling handmade baskets and other craft items, with Louisa even selling her illustrated poems.

By 1953, the two surviving sisters had tired of welcoming tourists, and they asked the park service to remove the sign directing visitors to their home. Margaret died in 1961, with Louisa following in 1964. For the first time since the early 1800s, no members of the Walker family lived in the hollers of the mountains.

Change is a constant in life, but people long for stability. For some, nostalgia is a way to cope with instability or feelings of helplessness in the face of uncontrollable change. It's a happy and comforting emotion, yet one tinged with sadness for times long past. Bert Walker probably felt unmoored from life on his farm in Drake Township and found solace in happier memories of life in Little Greenbrier.

Thomas Bert Walker died in Missouri in 1949. ✌

Chronicles of a
Young National Park
in the Smokies

1935 - 1968

Knoxville Tenn.
Aug. 8, 1933.

Dear Frank.

How are you by this time fine I hope this leves me O.K. But el can't get charley of my mind it sermes like he ought to be up thire with you. el gess it serms that way with you to. and you have been up thire with him so mush. I would like for you to come home friday But I gess you can't get to come home because pink is so sick I haven't seen you girls But I well talk for you when I see them. I have been having lomesome time down here. tell walter Hello for me and tell Earl I said I would like to see him. Jonnie B. said to be ofel carful. Arthur said to tell you Hello and he sow your Jine Sunday night. she is sweat has every and Black has every with Honey. I had better close for this time

so long tell I see you.

I love you little
I love you Big
I love you like
a little Pig

From Jewell
To my old Pal
Frank.

This letter from Jewell Maner to Frank Maples refers to the first tragedy to befall a Civilian Conservation Corps camp in the Smokies.

The Tragic Death of Charles Maner

1 9 3 3

Knoxville, Tenn.
Aug. 8, 1933

Dear Frank
How are you by this time fine I hope
this leves me O.K. But I can't get Charley of
my mind it semes like he ought to be up
thine with you. I gess it seme that way with
you to. And you have been up thine with him so
mush. I would like for you to come home Friday
But I gess you can't get to come home because
Pink is so sick I haven't seen you girls But I
well tolk for you when I see them. I have
been having lonesome time down here.
Tell Walter Hello from me and tell Earl I said
I would like to see him. Jonnie B. said to be
ofel carful. Arthur said to tell you Hello
and he saw your Jane Sunday night. She is
sweat has every and Black has every
well. Honey I had better close for this time.
So long till I see you.

I love you little
I love you big
I love you like
A little pig.

From Jewell
to my
old pal Frank.

Conceived in the depths of the Great Depression, the Civilian Conservation Corps (CCC) was one of many 'alphabet soup' New Deal programs designed to provide a jumpstart to a troubled economy and recovery to a damaged ecology. Authorized on March 21, 1933, as the Emergency Conservation Works (ECW), the CCC employed young, unmarried men between the ages of 18 and 25 who, due to their economic needs, qualified for public aid.

Enrollees in the program were paid $30 per month, with $25 of that being sent home to their families. In exchange, enrollees were put to work in national parks, state parks, and national forests to help build outdoor recreational infrastructure and to help mitigate years of ecological misuse and neglect. These men were housed in camps run by the US Army, with projects being managed by the Forest Service and the National Park Service, among others.

AX BLOW KILLS KNOX C. C. C. BOY

Charles Maner Cuts Artery in Leg; Body Returned Here; Lived at Powell's.

A young Knox Countian who went off to a reforestation camp is dead of an ax wound. The body of Charles Maner, 20, of Route 1, near Powells Station, today was at Weaver's funeral home. It was brought back last night from Newport, where he died in a hospital.

While young Maner was cutting timber near Camp Tyson, in the Cosby section of Cocke County yesterday, his ax struck his leg. An artery was severed.

He is survived by four brothers, Oscar and Glenn Maner of Sevierville, Roy and Arthur of Knoxville, Route 1; five sisters, Mrs. Grace Maples, Mrs. Emma Lee Large, Misses Mae, Anna and Jewell Maner of Knoxville.

The body was taken to the home of his sister, Mrs. Grace Maples, R. D. 1 The funeral party will leave the home at 11:30 a. m. Thursday for Vestal Baptist Church of Sevier County where services will be at 2 p. m. with the Rev. R. W. King officiating. Burial in church yard.

Maner is the third C. C. C. boy to be fatally injured this week. Leonard V. Williams of Holladay, Tenn., was killed by a hit-run driver while walking back to Camp McKellar at Morristown. Another hit-run driver struck two Tellico Plains boys from Camp Gleason, Kingsport, and one of them, Burlen Brown, died today at a Bristol hospital.

Knoxville News-Sentinel *article from August 2, 1933.*

Many of the young men admitted to the program were unprepared for their experience. Conditioning camps—where new enrollees spent two weeks before being transported to their permanent camps—reported that enrollees arrived suffering from undernourishment, illness, and general poor health. But soon, plentiful food, health care, exercise, and an atmosphere of abundance allowed them to achieve a level of physical and mental health that many had not experienced before. According to a report on the first enrollment period at GSMNP, "the close of the period revealed some fine physiques and coats of tan that would have been the envy of inhabitants of Florida or California."

Enrollees who served in NPS camps engaged in a wide variety of projects including campground and trail construction, reforestation, firefighting, and invasive species removal. During the first reporting period, enrollees in the Smokies removed fire hazards, built motorways and trails, constructed phone lines, and studied white pine blister rust, among other activities.

Much of the enrollees' work required the use of hand tools including shovels, axes, and sledgehammers. Due to the manual nature of the work, accidents were not uncommon. During the period between 1933 and 1942,

Post Exchange IOU. Less than a month before his death, Charles Maner borrowed 1 dollar against his next month's pay. CCC enrollees were paid a salary of $30 per month, $25 of which was sent home to help their struggling families.

CCC camps across the country reported 7,600 accidents to program headquarters in Washington, DC. This letter from Jewell Maner to Frank Maples refers to the first tragedy to befall a camp in the Smokies.

On August 1, 1933, while clearing brush on a hiking trail, Charles Maner cut his thigh with an axe. Maner, from Powell, Tennessee, was enrolled at Camp General Tyson, Cosby Creek, Tennessee. A tourniquet was applied to stanch the flow of blood, and Maner was able to make his way back to camp, by which time the bleeding had stopped. The camp doctor, Lt. Crowder, was called. In examining the wound, Crowder removed the bandage, taking with it a clot that had formed over the gash. The bleeding started again. Maner sat upright in his bed then fell back dead. Death was attributed to a coronary embolism.

Maner was one of nine children born to Mitchell and Mattie Maner, farmers in Jones Cove, Tennessee. After the death of Mitchell in 1923 and Mattie in 1930, the family scattered around the region. Before the widespread establishment of child welfare agencies, the death of a parent or guardian often caused the breakup of a large family. Many of the younger Maner children moved in with older siblings and their spouses. Charles and Jewell moved to Powell, Tennessee, with their older sister Grace, her husband, Pink Maples, and Pink's son, Frank. Frank would be enrolled at the same camp with Charles.

A week after Charles' death, still in shock over the loss of her older brother, 13-year-old Jewell wrote to her cousin Frank: "But I can't get Charley of my mind it semes like he ought to be up thine with you. I gess it semes that way with you to and you have been up thine with him so mush."

Though this was the first death in a CCC camp in the Smokies, it was not the last. During the nine years that the program operated in the park, there were numerous accidents and fatalities. Road construction was particularly hazardous. And in a freak accident near Bryson City, North Carolina, two enrollees died when a bus transporting 16 new recruits caught fire while it was being fueled.

The epitaph of English architect Sir Christopher Wren, designer of St. Paul's Cathedral, perhaps says it best: "Reader, if you seek his memorial, look around you." To see the works of the CCC, we need only look around us. It is in the trails, roads, forests, and buildings. That some gave their lives to this massive effort makes their contribution all the more powerful. ℰℐ

UNITED STATES
DEPARTMENT OF THE INTERIOR
NATIONAL PARK SERVICE
WASHINGTON

OFFICE OF THE DIRECTOR

December 4, 1935.

Col. D. C. Chapman,
    President, Great Smoky Mountains Conservation Association,
      516 State Street,
        Knoxville, Tennessee.

Dear Dave:

    I am sorry to have to tell you, in reply to your letter of December 2, that the possibility of a lake in Cades Cove is definitely out. We have found no justification for this based upon our standards. This does not mean, however, that we could not put in swimming pools as part of our future operations.

    The money that we have had from the Government toward the Great Smokies, $1,550,000, has been spent or obligated. Our estimates are that we will need about $700,000 more before we can complete the park. This is due to the tremendous excess in the awards in the Suncrest and Ravensford cases, and the additional appraisal costs of the land still unbought on the Tennessee side. This figure includes all the Aluminum Company of America lands. If we took only 5,000 acres we might get by with about a little over a half million dollars. Do you know where we could get the money?

    I was looking over last night some pictures that I took out at the old Annandale place. My heart ached when I saw them. I have never had the heart to go out on the place since it burned although I have viewed it from afar.

    Sincerely yours,

    Cam

    Arno B. Cammerer
    Director.

my best to Sue
+ Mrs. Saunders.

A Proposal for Cades Cove Lake

1 9 3 5

You might think that the creation of an artificial lake would be anathema to supporters of a proposed national park, but, as this letter shows, an artificial lake was indeed proposed in Cades Cove. The plan was to build a 60-foot-high dam across Abrams Creek to create a lake covering 1,196 acres, inundating the farms and structures of more than 40 former cove residents.

As early as 1926, members of the Southern Appalachian Parks Commission advocated for the creation of a lake in Cades Cove. Major William Welch, a member of the commission, was the first to propose the idea. Welch made the assertion that geologists had examined the valley and could easily see the outline of a former lake. Whether or not Welch's claim was a valid one, supporters latched onto the idea with a surprising amount of zeal. The pro-lake faction included the Great Smoky Mountains Conservation Association's founder, Col. David Chapman, and its board of trustees; Tennessee Governor

Fortunately for park visitors, a once-popular campaign to build a lake in Cades Cove ended in failure. In December 1935, National Park Service Director Arno B. Cammerer wrote to the Great Smoky Mountains Conservation Association's president, Col. David Chapman, to tell him that the lake would not be built, having "found no justification for this based upon our standards."

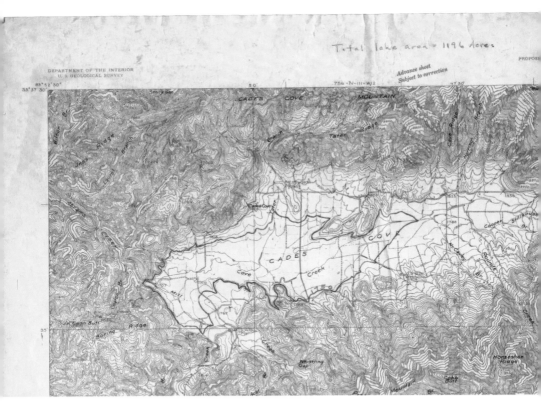

Total lake area = 1196 acres

Advance sheet
Subject to correction

Above: Map fragment showing the outline of the proposed 1,196-acre lake in Cades Cove. Right: The falls at Abrams Creek. In order to flood the cove, a dam would have been constructed on Abrams Creek.

Gordon Browning; and, surprisingly, then director of the National Park Service, Arno B. Cammerer.

Chapman, Welch, and Browning supported the lake because they saw an opportunity to place a jewel in the crown of Great Smoky Mountains National Park. They envisioned a beautiful mountain lake fed by crystal-clear waters and bounded by peaceful campgrounds. They believed the area would become a major destination for boaters, anglers, and those seeking a bucolic escape. Cammerer's support, however,

was more practical. He saw the creation of a lake as an expedient means of eliminating the presence of unsightly abandoned farmsteads in the valley.

Those opposed to the lake included Robert Sterling Yard, executive secretary of the National Parks Association and cofounder of the Wilderness Society; John C. Merriam, conservationist and cofounder of Save the Redwoods; Harvey Broome, Knoxville native and founding member of the Wilderness Society; and Benton MacKaye, conservationist and proponent of the

Appalachian Trail. In addition, the two previous directors of the National Park Service, Stephen Mather and Horace Albright, opposed the formation of the lake during their tenures.

In December 1933, the board of directors of the Great Smoky Mountains Conservation Association authorized a resolution in support of constructing a lake in the lower part of Cades Cove. The resolution described the area as "largely farmland." It addressed the argument that "the introduction of an artificial element into the Park would not constitute a restoration of a once-extant natural feature" by arguing the area was in no way primitive but had been under cultivation for generations. Rather, the lake would provide scientific value as a habitat for transient waterfowl and native game fish. In addition, it would provide a backdrop for a proposed tourist camp to be developed along its shore. Tellingly, the resolution failed to mention the possibility that a lake had existed there in the prehistoric past.

Ultimately the campaign to build a lake in Cades Cove collapsed. In December 1935, Cammerer wrote to Chapman to tell him that the lake would not be built, having "found no justification for this based upon our standards." The resolution failed for two reasons: Respected geologists—including Arthur Keith of the Appalachian Division of the Geological Survey—were unequivocal in their argument that at no time in the geological past had a lake existed in Cades Cove and, more importantly, the introduction of an artificial element of this scale would violate the ethos of the National Park Service.

However, the push to build a lake in the Smokies didn't end there. In 1937, Knoxville City Manager George Dempster renewed the call to build the lake. Dempster's association with a local construction firm that stood to profit from the construction project notwithstanding, the political pressure to sway the federal government didn't exist, and the last attempt to dam Abrams Creek died with a whimper. ✑

C O P Y

Cades Cove, Tenn.

Dec. 10, 1935.

Mr. Franklin D. Roosevelt:

Dear President.

I am writing you in regard to the condition that a number of us
familys in this country are in. We live in the great smoky mountains
national park. Some of us has lived here the most of our life. and for
the last few years we have leased from the park service. and now we
have received a notice to vacate by Jan. 1, 1936 so I have made all
eferts that I can to find somewhere to go and can not find no place
that i can get to rent that I can make a liven. All the farms is done
and retned. There is several familys and they have tried to get some
where to go to and can not. We have no money to by a place with and
we have no money to move with and if we are forced to move this winter
we will have to sell what little we have to live on now and it will
put us, our wives, and children on starviation for two years. It will
take what we have now and we cant get to make anything next year and we
no that our dear presidend has had mursey on the poor, and we hope that
you as our dear presidend will lend us a helping hand, if it lies in
your power. I plead that we may be alowed to lease for 1936 so we can
find somewhere that will not put our familys in distress. Thou noest that
times is hard and some of us has not had any work. I have not had only
about 8 months of work in the last 7 years. I have 3 children and have
made our liven threw this depression on the farm and there is more
familys in this place that is in just as hard luck as i am, and we beg the
mursey of our fedral goverment to have mursey on us and extend our
leases for 1936. if we are permitted to stay next year we will appreciate it very much and will sometime during the year vacate said
property. I am inclosing the notice that i received from Mr. J. R.
Eakin. I have not got to see Mr. Eakin yet but I am going to try to
get in tuch with him. Mr. Eakin and Mr. Dun has ben very good and kind
to us and i feal that if it lied in there power that they would help
us. We have been informed that these orders came from headquarters at
Washington, D. C. and that they could do nothing and that is why i am
writing you.

Our county judge our rural cariers, post masters, doctors, lawers,
preachers and anyone else in our county I think would sign a statement
that the peeple are not able to move now and that it would be better for
our state and county for the leases to be prolong another year. I am a
young preacher myself and i have been in the service of our lord and saviour
Jesus Christ near 4 years and i do testify to you that if we are all
forced to leafe this year that it will hurt in many ways. I understand
that there is over four hundred familys if i have not got the rong

---

*To soften the blow of losing their homes for the creation of Great Smoky Mountains
National Park, many homeowners were granted short-term leases to ease their transition
out of the park. But economic conditions resulting from the Great Depression coupled
with a fear of the unknown made some reluctant to leave. In this letter to President
Franklin Delano Roosevelt, Cades Cove resident W. B. Garland makes a plea for an
extension for his own family and many others.*

"Thou Noest That Times Is Hard"

1935

———— // ————

The creation of Great Smoky Mountains National Park is a well-known story to many. Local business leaders and regional boosters launched a protracted lobbying effort to convince the public and elected officials that the Southeast deserved a national park every bit as grand as those in the west—and the Great Smoky Mountains should be that new park's home.

But hundreds of families already called the mountains home. What about them?

The painful truth was, to establish the park, people would be dispossessed from their homes, communities wrenched apart, and traditional ways of life destroyed.* Though 'fair market value' was offered for properties, it was impossible to compensate people for the

---

* The history of forced displacement of people in the Smokies began long before the creation of the national park. The Cherokee people who have lived here for millennia were eventually forced off their ancestral homeland after years of duplicitous treatment by the colonial and later federal governments. This tragic saga culminated in the Indian Removal Act of 1830 and their subsequent violent removal to land in Oklahoma. On the route known as the Trail of Tears, thousands died of disease, starvation, and exposure before reaching their ultimate destination. Some Cherokee people, however, successfully resisted forced removal and managed to remain in the Smokies while others returned to the area from Oklahoma. Known as the Eastern Band of Cherokee Indians, they live primarily in the Qualla Boundary in Western North Carolina.

instruction that has bin notified to move and if this be true i hope
that there can be something done to protect our wives and children from
suffering.

Answer soon.

                  Yours truley

                    (Sgd) W. B. Garland

                          Cades Cove, Tenn.

        to your dearley beloved president

                  Mr. Franklin D. Roosevelt

may the blessing of god rest upon you. and the love of god ever keep,
comfert and strenging you in all your good deeds that you have done and will
do is my prayer to god.

*John W. Oliver, Cades Cove resident who
sued the state of Tennessee over its use of
eminent domain.*

The John W. Oliver home in Cades Cove, Tennessee.

hard work, heartache, and joy poured into their mountain homes.

Nevertheless, most took the proffered money and made new lives outside the mountains. Others found the transition more difficult.

For those who needed additional support, Tennessee National Park Commission Chair David Chapman proposed a lifeline of sorts. Some residents were offered short-term, low-cost leases until they could secure homes outside the park. While others, notably the elderly or infirm, were given lifetime leases, allowing them to live out their remaining years in their family homes.

The Walker sisters of Little Greenbrier in Tennessee were granted a lifetime lease and lived on their property until the last sister, Louisa, died there in 1964.

Leasing eased the sting of dislocation from home and community but came with numerous caveats and restrictions. Property owners were expected to settle for a reduced purchase price for their land. In exchange, they paid an annual rent, no more than

518

Park enemies in Cades Cove put this sign up (March 1928) as part of their campaign of abuse and obstruction. It reads: "Col. Chapman you and hoast are notify let the Cove people alone Get out Get gone 40 M limit." (The "40 M" refers to the distance between Knoxville and Cades Cove.)

Photographed — Carlos C. Campbell — Mch. 9, 1935   #518

Motivated by animosity towards the National Park Service, an unknown person posted this sign on the road leading into Cades Cove in 1928. "Col. Chapman you and hoast are notify let the cove people alone. Get out. Get gone 40m limit."

a few dollars for most, and could stay on their land for one or two years. These leases were often extended beyond the initial term but would not be renewed once the park began to develop trails and other visitor amenities in the area.

On top of that, a lease didn't cover the entire area sold to the park commission. It was limited to the land currently under the plow and to the buildings required to run the farm. While farming could continue, a change in crops had to be approved by the superintendent's office, and no previously untilled land could be turned over.

Moreover, no timber could be cut, structures removed, or livestock grazed. Meanwhile, leaseholders were expected to assist in fighting wildfires. Hunting was prohibited, and fishing required a license and adherence to state and federal regulations. Making whiskey and other illegal activities were grounds for immediate expulsion from the park.

All the while, the Tennessee National Park Commission had no legal authority to issue leases, and the National Park Service was under no obligation to honor them. But just as the park commission believed that offering leases was a mercy, the park service felt bound to honor them as long as was practical.

The park commission also believed that offering leases to ease the tran-

sition would make property owners who hadn't been approached yet less inclined to fight the inevitable. Those who did contest the seizure of their land were much less likely to be offered an affordable lease. The park's first superintendent, Ross Eakin, was not generous to those who resisted the coming of change. He believed that "leases for land should not be issued to those who were antagonistic to the park."

John Oliver of Cades Cove, for instance, discovered just how implacable Eakin could be. In 1929, Oliver sued the state over its use of eminent domain to seize private land. The suit stirred up resentment against the park and drove a wedge between neighbors. After several years in the court system, however, justices ruled in favor of the state, and Oliver was forced to sell his land.

In 1934, Oliver, who farmed and delivered mail in the cove, was offered a lease in the amount of $1,020 per year. This was dramatically higher than offers to his neighbors. When Oliver pointed this out, Eakin offered to reduce the amount to $60 annually. Insulted even by this amount, Oliver gave notice that he would vacate the property as soon as possible.

The park service also reserved the right to cancel a lease with little notice if the lease holder violated park regulations. In late 1935, Claude Gregory, the 17-year-old son of William Gregory of Cades Cove, was accused by the superintendent of the CCC camp of illegally harvesting apples from the Tipton orchard. Claude confessed and returned the apples. According to the complaint, Claude was so angry that he set fire to a field before driving out of the cove. A week later, Eakin sent the senior Gregory a letter informing him that, because his boys could not be controlled, the family must vacate the park by the end of the year.

Farm families weren't the only ones to receive leases. Many people owned vacation properties in the mountains. Elkmont, an enclave of vacation homes built by prosperous East Tennesseans on the Little River, was exempted from the state's use of eminent domain. Money and political savvy allowed property owners there to successfully negotiate sales to the park commission that allowed them lifetime leases, guaranteeing them access to their properties until the 1990s.

In North Carolina, leases were less common. Most residents moved almost as soon as their properties were purchased, and few sought to return. It quickly became evident, however, that help was needed to fight wildfires and to keep up the vacated cabins that would be converted into permanent homes for district rangers. To this end,

Chief Ranger John Needham sought out local people who could be relied upon to aid with fire control and to occupy and maintain selected properties. These were rarely the original owners but were nonetheless valued for their trustworthiness and competence.

World War II brought a halt to development in the park and with it a more relaxed view of leases and extensions. The end of the war, though, saw a return to park development as well as a change in management. David Chapman died in 1944, and with his passing, many still living in the park lost a champion. In 1945, a stroke forced Ross Eakin to retire from the park service.

The new management, headed by Superintendent Fred Overly, and new leadership in Washington were eager to get on with the business of building a park. Administrators were no longer lenient in considering lease extensions; those claiming lifetime leases were expected to demonstrate the legitimacy of their claims. By the late 1940s, all but a handful of leases were terminated.

Without question, the creation of Great Smoky Mountains National Park took a monumental effort. A vast expenditure of capital was invested in purchasing hundreds of tracts of land. And while a dollar figure can be placed on that, there can never be an adequate accounting of the lives that were changed in the process. Communities were destroyed, families were scattered, and people were driven into the greater world. Many prospered, some struggled, but all were changed. ✦

August 16, 1937 -
Glenbrook, Conn.

Dear Maida & Doug,

The calendar says that your trip is half over - that's too bad - and ours is all over - worse luck.

I wonder if you received our cards - sent to Seattle, Portland, and San Francisco - also 'a telegram' to your train in New York? A card from Ing said that she was expecting to see you in Banff. Did you see her? Did you happen to see the town "Greeley" in Colorado? Several teachers I know have been there to school this summer.

Our trip was pretty nice we thought. We drove 2377 miles in all - 1,000 down, 930 back and the rest around the Smoky

---

The experiences this Connecticut couple wrote about of their vacation in the new national park in 1937 will be familiar to those who visit the park today.

Such Sunsets
Out of Our Windows

1937

———— *l* ————

When Zora and William Collins visited the Smokies in 1937, they arrived on the crest of a great wave of change. The region was on the cusp of growth and development not seen since the coming of the railroads in the 19th century. Good roads, a national park, and the tourist dollar were about to make the Smokies one of the biggest travel destinations in Southern Appalachia.

This letter from Zora to her sister- and brother-in-law, Maida and Doug Seelye, is a brief travelogue of the Collinses' trip to the Smokies. Though written decades ago, visitors today will find much that is familiar.

The Connecticut couple, he an auto mechanic and she a schoolteacher in the Greenville Connecticut Public School System, were the perfect tourists for the as-yet-incomplete national park.

Their visit heralded a new era in tourism that the region was finally ready for: the motor tourist.

Tourism itself was nothing new in Southern Appalachia. The 'salubrious' climate drew people to the many resorts and inns that dotted the region before and after the Civil War. Western North Carolina was especially renowned for holiday destinations catering to outdoor enthusiasts.

Then, in the early 20th century, the logging industry took advantage of the beautiful scenery to entice tourists into the Smokies. The rail lines that carried timber out of the mountains brought vacationers in. Special excursion trains conveyed well-heeled pleasure seekers, along with their automobiles, to destinations like the exclusive vacation enclave of Elkmont, Tennessee.

Mountains. We stayed 4 days at Onitaluga Inn near Bryson City, N.C. We were very comfortable there and had excellent food, - even to having "mountain dew" served by our host.

The Hewitts were with us from Monday afternoon until Sat. A.M. Ruth and Paul stayed at the inn two days longer after we left.

Before the Hewitts left, we had a fine trip of 200 miles up through the New Found Gap, up Clingman's Dome — The roads are fine — such curves, with no fences or stone walls — We then crossed over into Tennessee for a long ways.

It was very interesting riding around the Cherokee Indian Reservation — We had quite a talk with one family — I've a good

Later, as cars became more affordable and ownership proliferated among the middle class, adventure seekers from Knoxville, Tennessee, and Asheville, North Carolina, began exploring places like Cades Cove and Cataloochee Valley. But braving the mountains on unpaved wagon trails underscored the need for hard-surface, all-weather roads throughout the region.

While well-maintained roads were more common in the North, the

snapshot of them. We went to a pageant on Sunday afternoon, telling the life of the tribe. I guess all Indians were pretty badly treated by the white men.

Saturday night we were fortunate to see some real mountain dances — with a real hill-billy band.

On our ride we stopped at an inn to have some coffee as it was rainy & cool — We saw many mountaineers trying to roller skate — How hard they tried. They fell down every other minute. The owner of that inn certainly is making money on that scheme.

We drove home in 3 days, leaving at 6 a.m. Monday — I stayed awake all night to be sure to be awake on time. It was dark when we left. We saw a beautiful sunrise later on. (and such sunsets out of our windows facing Clingman's Dome sometimes — the clouds were way

South lagged behind. As the economic benefits of good roads became apparent, thousands of citizens in the South, including those in Tennessee and North Carolina, joined local Good Roads associations to lobby state legislators to build and maintain public roadways.

Knoxville and Asheville became vital hubs for the growth of roads in the Southeast, with each city hosting chapters of various motoring clubs.

below the visible mountain tops.)
We drove 397 mi. the 1st day and
about 270 the other two. It grew
hotter as we left the mts. It was
very hot & sticky here all the while
we were away. Our flowers are
still very nice. The dahlias & "glads"
are out, also the petunias are very
pretty!

Grandpa appears to be a little
better — Grace had more teeth out
& was sick a week or so — just after
the lightning struck the barn — We
expected the Reels down Sunday but
Nellie was sick suddenly — Beatrice is
quite ill — was in hospital 2 weeks.
We saw Christine Blackburn last
night at the Chalmers — She was the
girl who drove to Columbia with me —
She is going to school this summer too —
They all are coming over to-night —
the Senfts will be up to-morrow —
Mrs. Viele was over this A. M — Peter
had just been vaccinated — in return for
his promise not to cry, Peter got an icecream
soda, trip to the movies & 5¢ worth of candy
to eat at the movies. Then the vaccination
didn't take. I know what a grand time you're having.
Come down soon & tell us all about it before you get all
talked out. Much love from us — Zoe

GRSM 108629a

Mrs. W. J. Collins
Holmes Ave.
Glenbrook, Conn.

STAMFORD
AUG 26
5 30 PM
CONN.
1931

Mrs. Douglas Seelye
Hotel Clark
Los Angeles
California

902

122

Organizations such as the American Automobile Association (AAA) and the East Tennessee Automobile Club (ETAC) promoted auto tourism. As the park movement gained momentum, both cities pointed drivers to the new national park.

It's no coincidence that, in 1924, the Great Smoky Mountains Conservation Association (GSMCA) was founded in the same office as the East Tennessee Automobile Club. Knoxville business leader Willis Davis was appointed president of the GSMCA, and the entire board of the ETAC served on the board of the new conservation association.

Business leaders and local elected officials alike appreciated the federal government's proposal to establish Great Smoky Mountains National Park. In 1929, North Carolina Governor Max Gardner said of the park: "This wonderland of our mountain region may be saved for the enjoyment of our people and the nation." And that's exactly what the Collinses and thousands of others were doing in 1937, enjoying the park and the mountain communities that surrounded it.

But where would people stay when they visited?

According to general information released by the park superintendent's office in Gatlinburg in 1937, "The park is at present in the 'proposed' stage and no developments such as buildings and tourist camps, the establishment of ranger-naturalist guide services and other similar developments for the convenience of the traveler, have as yet taken place."

In a 1937 article in the *Asheville Citizen-Times*, the lack of lodging in the park made it desirable "exclusively to motor tourists—people who have accommodations for lodging outside the park and motor through in their cars or sightseeing buses. The highways in the park are excellent and they were built so as to make it possible for motorists to get maximum enjoyment out of the park without so much as getting out of their seats if they don't want to."

The park service estimated that 95 percent of people who visited wanted nothing more than a pleasant scenic drive, even though 800 miles of trails wound through the park.

A lack of amenities certainly didn't deter visitors. In 1936, more than 602,000 people visited the park, and an estimated 744,000 were expected the following year. Except for the war years, when gasoline and tire rationing made travel difficult, visitation increased almost every year, growing to an astonishing 14 million visitors in 2021. By the mid-1930s, tourism was a $5 billion industry nationwide. To get a slice of that economic pie, North Carolina added an advertising division to its Department of Conservation and Development. This effort, combined with the governor's hospitality committee, enticed tourists to spend more than $50 million in 1938, equal to the value of all the cotton and one-third of the tobacco grown in the state.

However, because of racial segregation, the White middle-class tourist dollar was prized above all others. African Americans still visited the region for leisure but were severely restricted in where they could lodge, eat, and recreate. This situation would take decades to change.

☙ ☙ ☙

The Collinses probably weren't concerned about a lack of development in the park. They stayed for several days at the Onitaluga Inn near Bryson City, North Carolina, and enjoyed the hospitality the region is yet known for. They ate good food, listened to mountain music, and even sampled 'moonshine'—many of the same things people look forward to today

Bryson City and other gateway communities willingly catered to travelers headed to the mountains. Hotels, restaurants, and myriad entertainment venues developed and continue to serve tourists' needs in the region.

An unidentified couple taking in the sunset from Clingmans Dome Observation Tower, May 16, 1938.

The Eastern Band of Cherokee Indians (EBCI) in the Qualla Boundary in North Carolina were well-positioned for the new influx of vacationers. As far back as 1914, at the urging of the Bureau of Indian Affairs, the EBCI began developing its own tourism industry. The Cherokee Indian Fair, first held in 1914, highlighted traditional Cherokee agriculture, crafts, and culture—and was a major tourist attraction by the 1950s.

Another attraction attended by the Collinses was the *Spirit of the Great Smokies* pageant dramatizing the history of the EBCI from earliest contact with Spanish colonists to the modern era. More than 350 people took part in each production. In 1950, a new interpretation of EBCI history was launched with the first production of *Unto These Hills*, which is still performed today.

In all, the Collinses drove 447 miles through the mountains. Zora wrote to her sister of their trip to Clingmans Dome, "The roads are fine—such curves, with no fences or stone walls—we then crossed over into Tennessee for a long way." On their return to Connecticut she continued,

"It was dark when we left. We saw a beautiful sunrise later on (and such sunsets out of our windows facing Clingmans Dome, sometimes the clouds were way below the visible mountain tops)."

ᎤᎧ ᎤᎧ ᎤᎧ

In 1938, the park emerged from "proposed" status when President Franklin D. Roosevelt signed the Second Deficiency Bill for the 75th Congress, which contained funds to complete the park. Modern campground construction began, with other developments soon following.

World War II interrupted tourism in Southern Appalachia, as well as development in the park, but both came

The town of Cherokee, North Carolina, in the Qualla Boundary, began welcoming tourists to the area as early as 1914. Seen here in 1940, the town is still a major tourist destination.

roaring back in the 1950s.

It's been over 80 years since Zora and William Collins visited Great Smoky Mountains National Park. Would they recognize the area today?

Certainly, there have been many changes. Campgrounds, visitor centers, ranger programs, roads, and trails have all been fully developed. Over time, the diligent work of park employees and new environmental protections have helped clear the air and clean the water, supporting the park's world-renowned biodiversity.

The sleepy little communities the couple encountered in 1937 are bursting these days with hotels, restaurants, tourist attractions—and the money those tourists bring. Billions of dollars flood into the region annually. Tourism is now the area's single largest economic driver.

But some of the key things the Collinses found in the mountains remain unchanged. The mountains themselves are invariable

Even before it was dedicated, visitors could see the park from the comfort of special touring coaches, like this one from the Smoky Mountain Taxi Company, seen here at Chimneys Campground in 1935.

in their appeal. Those original mountaineers have been succeeded by their
children and their children's children,
who retain the same grace and open
friendliness of their forebears. As well,
the Cherokee people continue to share
their culture with new generations
of visitors. After all these years, the
beauty and charm that drew so many
visitors to the Smokies then—and continue to draw millions each year—are
unwavering. ❧

PHONE 2111

LECONTE LODGE

"6,593 FEET INTO THE CLOUDS"

GREAT SMOKY MOUNTAINS NATIONAL PARK

GATLINBURG, TENNESSEE

July 17, 1940

Superintendent J. R. Eakin
 Gatlinburg, Tenn.

Dear Superintendent:

Meeting some ten thousand people in seven months, one is surley to meet some
that are out of place are a little bit on the soar side.

I am very sorrow that such ocaasions as the one with Miss Margret and Mary
Shlinding had to happen. It makes our work and the whole camp unpleasant. I am
sorrow again that they simpley told the story all wrong. I took the two ladiesinto
the lodge and built them a fire. After that they ask me for whiskey and I told
them that the State of Tennessee was still dry. Then they ask me for Coffee. I told
them that I only served coffee with meals. At that they left the lodge and the
fire burned up without anyone using it or any thanks for building it.

The ladies were not any guest of mine.

I hardly see how that I insulted them when the only words I spoke were,
"Come into this cabin please,""the state of Tennessee was still dry," and "I
only serve Coffee with meals".

Iffyou wish me to serve the thing people ask for such as Coffee, Whisker,
beer, candy and such I would like to build a building for that end as the people
of that tipe would ruin my buisness in the lodge. If one expects to hafe a buisness one must take care of it.

What we need here now:
 A reseption hall, toilet facilities, two more lodges like the one we have
now and a house for storage.

What can be done about people coming into camp and didterbing our guests
late at night? That happened last night and several times this year.

Yiurs truly,

Jack Huff

Jack Huff

JUL 23 1940

128

Balancing Act on Mount Le Conte

1940

———————— *11* ————————

Managing a public concession in a national park can be a challenging endeavor. Shifting park policies, anticipating the needs of guests, and trying to build a successful business can all come into conflict. And when attempting all this on top of an isolated mountain peak in Southern Appalachia accessible only on foot or horseback, the demands only multiply.

Those were the challenges faced by LeConte Lodge owner Jack Huff. Established in 1925 through an arrangement between the Great Smoky Mountain Conservation Association and the Champion Fibre Company, which owned Mount Le Conte, the lodge was used by park boosters to build support for a national park in Southern Appalachia.

The first structure, built by Paul Adams and Will Ramsay, was a large, crude lean-to made of balsam logs with a canvas roof. The lodge's first guests were a group of 15 people including NPS Director Arno B. Cammerer, park booster Harlan P. Kelsey, and GSMCA President Col. David Chapman.

In July 1940, Margaret and Mary Selinding, visiting from Petersburg, Illinois, discovered just how spare day-tripper accommodations were on Mount Le Conte. Having ridden their horses to LeConte Lodge in a downpour, the two weary travelers approached Huff and inquired after shelter, a warm fire, and a cup of coffee. In a subsequent letter to GSMNP Superintendent Ross Eakin, the two claimed they were refused entry to the lodge and that Huff's actions "were almost, if not quite, insulting."

2479

Top: Pauline and Jack Huff, winter 1937. The Huffs managed the lodge on Mount Le Conte for more than 35 years. In that time, their names became synonymous with the highest guest lodge in the eastern United States and the only lodge in GSMNP. Left: Andrew Jackson "Jack" Huff in 1926, the year after the first cabin at LeConte Lodge was built.

Seen here in 1940, LeConte Lodge grew to include outhouses, cabins, a kitchen, and a main lodge that guests still visit today.

LeConte Lodge quickly became an important tourist destination known for its views of unsurpassed beauty.

Early on, the lodge lacked even the most basic of amenities, including adequate sanitation facilities. Meals weren't included in the price of a bed, though some basic supplies could be purchased from the proprietor, and only an outdoor kitchen and communal dining table were available for the guests to use.

As visitation increased, Huff, who took over management of the lodge in 1926, added conveniences such as outhouses, cabins, and prepared meals. While most of the additions catered to the needs of overnight guests, the casual day hiker who stopped at the lodge found little in the way of such comforts.

In July 1940, Margaret and Mary Selinding, visiting from Petersburg, Illinois, discovered just how spare day-tripper accommodations were. Having ridden their horses to LeConte Lodge in a downpour, the two weary travelers approached Huff and inquired after shelter, a warm fire, and a cup of coffee. In a subsequent letter to GSMNP Superintendent Ross Eakin, the two claimed they were refused entry to the lodge and that Huff's actions "were almost, if not quite, insulting." Eakin then wrote to Huff, upbraiding him for his poor manners and reminding him that being in the hospitality industry required him to see that his visitors "are treated courteously and helpfully."

In his own defense, Huff claimed he *did* try to accommodate their needs. "I took the two ladies into the lodge and built them a fire. After that they ask me for whiskey and I told them that the State of Tennessee was still dry. Then they ask me for coffee. I told them that I only served coffee with meals. At that they left the lodge and the fire burned up without anyone using it or any thanks for building it."

For Huff, the problem lay in guests who expected to enjoy his hospitality without having to pay for it. "The ladies were not any guest of mine," Huff wrote. His solution was to build a separate structure to sell "coffee, whisker [sic], beer, candy, and such," as without it the "people of that

tipe [sic] would ruin my business in the lodge." And while the park was reticent to allow Huff to expand the existing footprint of the camp, they did encourage him to sell coffee, sandwiches, and candy bars as a way of accommodating day hikers while increasing his profits.

Making a profit on Mount Le Conte was not easy. During the first several decades of the camp's operation, Huff and his wife, Pauline, often worked each day of the operating season without taking a salary themselves. In the early 1950s, Huff even approached the Department of the Interior to request permission to operate a 40-to-50-room hotel in Cades Cove simply as a means of continuing to run LeConte Lodge rather than selling it as an unprofitable endeavor.

Though complaints continued to plague Huff—his inhospitable demeanor and the quality of the food on offer chief among them—there were just as many compliments made to his hospitality and overall well-run operation. Carlos Campbell, secretary of the GSMCA, defended Huff, saying, "I think Jack has rendered a fine service and at a very nominal cost to the public."

Despite the difficulty of operating a concession on one of the highest peaks in the park, Huff and his wife managed the lodge until 1960, when they finally sold to a couple from Knoxville. The Huffs ran LeConte for nearly 40 years. Though it was sometimes a bumpy ride, they left a lasting impression on tens of thousands of visitors and helped build a lodge with a reputation that still serves hikers today. ❧

4101 – 36th N. E.
Seattle 5, Wn.
August 11, 1953

Mr. Arthur Stupka
Great Smoky National Park
Gatlinburg, Tennessee

Dear Mr. Stupka:

The Grand Tour is about over. James Fisher has returned to
England and I am starting from from Seattle with Barbara and
the boys tomorrow.

Our total list of species came to about 600---530 north of the
Mexican border which beats Guy Emerson's record of 497 for a
year's list. This is pretty good considering we were not
specifically out for just a list. By going out of our way and
sacrificing other things we might have added another 20.

I took probably 7,000 feet of film some of which you will certainly see when I get it whipped into shape for the Screen Tours.

The trip was terrific but at times sort of a rat race. In the
effort to keep on schedule we often turned in quite late and our
journals may have suffered somewhat. Now for the first time in
months I can get at my correspondence.

I wish to thank you again for your generous hospitality and for
acting as our guide while we were in the park. The trees made a
tremendous impression on Mr. Fisher. We were fortunate also to
get the flood tide of warblers just about that point. Next time
I come to the Smokies I shall stay there awhile.

With best wishes,

                            Sincerely,

                            Roger T. Peterson

                            Roger T. Peterson

Two for the Road

1 9 5 3

———————

In May 1953, two legendary naturalists on an epic road trip to view the natural wonders of America swung through the Great Smoky Mountains. Their 100-day, 30,000-mile journey brought them face-to-face with the ecological diversity of a changing American landscape and helped to usher in a wave of conservation efforts from which we still benefit today.

When Roger Tory Peterson, celebrated ornithologist, artist, and author of the first easy-to-use birding book, *A Field Guide to the Birds,* invited his friend James Fisher to America to "conduct him around the continent," it was by way of repaying a bit of hospitality.

From Britain, Fisher was the preeminent expert on European seabirds, an authority on English naturalist Gilbert White, and a celebrity naturalist featured regularly on the BBC. Peterson and Fisher had met several years earlier and frequently traveled together, spying out nesting sites in Norway, Sweden, Scotland, and the Mediterranean and observing and recording hundreds of avian species.

Peterson arranged to meet Fisher in Nova Scotia in April 1953. After several delays, Fisher arrived, and the two loaded binoculars, cameras, field guides, and journals into Peterson's station wagon and hit the road. The journey took

---

From one great naturalist to another, this 1953 letter from Roger Tory Peterson thanks Ranger Naturalist Arthur Stupka for his hospitality and expertise. Peterson and English ornithologist James Fisher stopped in the Smokies during their whirlwind tour of the United States.

Above: James Fisher (third from the left) and Roger Tory Peterson (second from the right) on Mousa Island, Scotland, 1961. Image courtesy of Roger Tory Peterson Institute. Right: Arthur Stupka's observation notes for April 1953, crediting Fisher and Peterson with sighting the first laughing gull in GSMNP.

20

APRIL, 1953, BIRDS (Some)

B - Buckhorn	LC - Laurel Creek
CC - Cades Cove	LL - Laurel Lake
FCG- Fighting Creek Gap	LR - Little River
G - Gatlinburg	NG - Newfound Gap
GP - Grassy Patch	ORS- Oconaluftee Ranger Station
H - Headquarters	PF - Pigeon Forge
IG - Indian Gap	Sug- Sugarlands
ULR- Upper Little River	T - Tuckaleechee Cove

Pied-billed Grebe - Little Pigeon R. (half-way between G and
 PF), Apr. 8 - 1 bird; LL, Apr. 30 (1 bird)
Pintail - Between G and H, Apr. 14 (1 drake on river - J. Manley)
Blue-winged Teal - Little Pigeon R., between H and G, Apr. 28
 (6 birds - J. Manley); LL, Apr. 30 (5 birds)
Scaup - LL, Apr. 30 (a few)
Ruddy Duck - LL, Apr. 30 (1 bird)
Turkey Vulture - FCG; LR; H
Sharp-shinned Hawk - PF, Apr. 21 (J. Manley)
Red-tailed Hawk - LR, Apr. 28
Broad-winged Hawk - ULR, Apr. 16; G, Apr. 14 (J. Manley); H; NG,
 Apr. 29 (2 birds)
Osprey - Mth Abrams Cr., Apr. 14 (Don Pfitzer)
Ruffed Grouse - LC
Bob White - B, Apr. 30
Turkey - Cre, Apr. 22 (1 bird near old CCC Camp - J. Morrell)
Coot - LL, Apr. 30 (25-30 birds)
Spotted Sandpiper - Sug, Apr. 22 (1 bird - 1st of yr.); LL, Apr.
* Laughing Gull - Mt. Rd., N.C. (U.S. 441) near Kephart Prong -
 Apr. 30 - 1 bird perched close to rd. where it
 was observed about 8:00 a.m. by Roger Tory Peter
 son and James Fisher (Britain); Peterson, who
 reported it to me, was inclined to the belief
 that recent storms and high winds in So. States
 was probably a factor: 1st Park record (Record
 in Knoxville in 1932)
Screech Owl - B, Apr. 5 (1 red-colored bird dead in rd. at jct.
 1/2 mile from our house - in its stomach I found
 17 small moths and 6 lepid. larvae); G, Apr. 24
 (1 red-colored adult + 2 eggs + 2 young birds
 brought to local school by a child - Mr. Manley,
 who is attempting to rear the young, estimated
 their age at 7 to 8 days).
Whip-poor-will - B, Apr. 3; Ravensford, Apr. 1 (1st of yr. -
 heard in early a.m. by Ranger Ealy)
Chimney Swift - B and H, Apr. 9; G, Apr. 8 (1st of yr. - J. Manl
Hummingbird - G, Apr. 14 (J. Manley); B, Apr. 24; H; T
Kingfisher - G; ORS; H
Flicker - H; ORS; B; LL

them down the East Coast, across the South to Mexico, up through the Rocky Mountains, and across to the West Coast, ending 100 days later in Alaska.

Barely five weeks into their travels, the pair motored down the Blue Ridge Parkway and crossed into Great Smoky Mountains National Park. They were greeted with an experience typical of the Smokies; rain and thick clouds shrouded their drive through the Qualla Boundary and up to Newfound Gap, their first stop in the park.

They had arrived on the heels of a major storm that had blown in from the Atlantic. Wind and rain weren't the only things carried in on the storm. Fisher was shocked to see a laughing gull (*Leucophaeus atricilla*) resting on a bar of gravel on the side of the highway near Clingmans Dome. The naturalists believed the bird had been blown off course by the storm and, mistaking the gravel for a stretch of sea beach, stopped to rest before flying 300 miles back to the ocean. Later that day, park naturalist Arthur Stupka confirmed this as a first sighting of a laughing gull in the Smokies.

Over the next two days, Peterson and Fisher explored the park with Stupka and Ranger Naturalist Glidden Baldwin. Arriving at the height of the migration of hundreds of warblers through the park, Fisher wrote in his journal, "Warblers, warblers, everywhere, nor any time to think."

On a hike up Ramsey Cascades Trail, Fisher was awestruck by the enormity and variety of trees he encountered. He would later write, "Near the beginning of the trail a tulip tree towered higher than any tree I had ever seen in Britain; and from then on big trees of at least six kinds thrust up from the tangled forest floor for about a hundred feet, or more."

After sampling wild ramps and finding a red-cheeked salamander under a downed log but failing to locate a saw-whet owl, the duo returned and spent the night with the Stupkas. Fisher later remarked that the Smokies were the most beautiful forest he'd ever seen. The pair were on the road the next morning and would eventually view a broad swath of flora and fauna across America, all before the advent of interstate highways, GPS, or air-conditioned motoring comfort.

Two years after their whirlwind tour of North America, they released the book *Wild America: The Legendary Story of Two Great Naturalists on the Road*. Comprised of daily journal entries, primarily those of Fisher, and punctuated with Peterson's artwork, the book joined a growing list of important environmental writings that helped promote the conservation of the natural world to the American public.

Book-ended by Aldo Leopold's *A Sand County Almanac*, published in

1949, and Rachel Carson's ground-breaking 1962 release *Silent Spring*, these observations and others helped to propel the conservation movement into the global consciousness. The result was a series of groundbreaking government actions that helped stem the tide of ecological decline in the postwar era. Many of these actions were vital in restoring and protecting natural areas, including the Wilderness Act (1964), the National Environmental Policy Act (1969), the Clean Air Act (1970), the Clean Water Act (1972), and the Endangered Species Act (1974).

Since the naturalists' 1953 visit, the park has made some amazing advances in conservation. Peregrine falcons, which had been entirely wiped out in the eastern United States by 1965, began making a comeback in the late 1990s. As written about by Carson, widespread use of the insecticide DDT had caused a rapid decline in the falcon population. But the banning of DDT in 1972, combined with a captive breeding program and a hatching technique called "hacking," where a falcon chick is raised in special enclosures on a high precipice, resulted in the first falcon to hatch in the Smokies in 1997.

Other conservation success stories include the historic reintroduction of elk in 2001, the return from near extinction of the native catfish known as the Smoky madtom, and the restoration of the Southern Appalachian brook trout, the only trout species native to the Smokies. The unsuccessful reintroduction of the red wolf stands out as a singular failure in the park's efforts at conservation.

Astonishingly, the Smokies are home to 240 species of birds, including 60 permanent species and 120 breeding species. But since the mid-20th century, climate change and habitat loss have decreased the global bird population by nearly three billion, meaning more than one in four birds has disappeared from the earth.

Each year, millions of visitors explore the wonders of Great Smoky Mountains National Park. Events like the Annual Spring Wildflower Pilgrimage and the Audubon Christmas Bird Count draw thousands to the park. But without the dedicated work of naturalists and conservationists who study our interconnected web of life, there would be far fewer of these natural wonders to experience.

☙ ☙ ☙

Several years after their adventure, Peterson and Fisher had planned to recreate portions of their *Wild America* trip for a four-part American television program. But Fisher's death in an automobile accident in 1970 halted the project. Peterson died in 1996 at his home in Old Lyme, Connecticut. ☙

Top: Roger Tory Peterson, Bass Rock, Scotland, 1961. Image courtesy Roger Tory Peterson Institute. Bottom: James Fisher. Image courtesy National Portrait Gallery, United Kingdom.

George Fry -

Go away, Leave, Resign,
Vamoose, Transfer,
Any thing just so
you go go go -

We don't want you
any longer, We
much prefer the
Bear, They are
not half as
dangerous.

Two Native

Sevier Countians

A Plan to Beat and Banish Bears

1 9 6 8

Managing human–bear interactions has been a challenge for the National Park Service from its earliest days. In the 1940s, rangers at Yosemite National Park, in an attempt to lure food-conditioned bears away from campgrounds and other populated areas, established a feeding program for the valley's black bears.

Food waste was provided for these bears in an isolated location at the far end of the valley. However, rather than lure the bears from the populated areas, it further habituated them to human food and provided a spectacle for park visitors. In the Smokies, it was common for visitors to take food to the Chimneys Campground or the pull-outs along Highway 441 and spend the afternoon feeding the local bears.

But in 1967, events occurred at Glacier National Park that impacted national park units across the country and changed the way park management

A new bear management plan reported in the Knoxville News-Sentinel *on April 21, 1968, stated that the plan involved "removing bears on first appearance, from the Chimneys and Elkmont Camp Grounds and along US 441 at park headquarters and Newfound Gap." This led readers to believe that all bears, not just those seeking human food, would be removed from the park. The article went on to claim that bears would be hit with clubs to instill a fear of humans in them. Management didn't spell out what aversion method would be used, so the source of this information is unclear.*

DANGEROUS

BEARS are wild animals. They may look tame, but many injuries to visitors show that they are not. Enjoy watching them at a safe distance. Pull off the road, and stay in your car. To protect you, it is necessary to enforce the regulation that prohibits feeding or molesting bears.

16—63682-1   GPO

NATIONAL PARK SERVICE
United States Department of the Interior

approached human–bear relations. Two women, several miles apart, were fatally mauled by grizzly bears. The factors that led to those deaths—bears' ready access to human food and the resulting decreased fear of humans—were evident in any national park that had a bear population, including the Smokies. The tragic events that summer reverberated throughout the National Park Service and resulted in a sea change in NPS bear-management policy.

Immediately following the deaths at Glacier, NPS units began to re-examine their bear policies. In January 1968, GSMNP Chief Ranger G. Lee Sneddon released to Superintendent George Fry a revised bear-management program for the Smokies. Approved in March 1968, the program outlined a two-pronged approach to bear manage-ment: control of people and control of bears. Zones of control were established around campgrounds, visitor centers, and the Tennessee side of Highway 441—and these areas were targeted for vigilant application of the new policy.

Controlling bears' access to human food was relatively straightforward. Improved bear-resistant trash cans were installed in the campgrounds and highway pullouts, and trash pickup was increased. In the backcountry, entrances to overnight shelters were fenced off, and bear-resistant food caches were installed at some of them. In con-junction, an intense public education campaign about the dangers of feeding wildlife was rolled out. Posters, media engagement, and interpretive program-ming informed visitors about stricter enforcement of existing laws. It was also

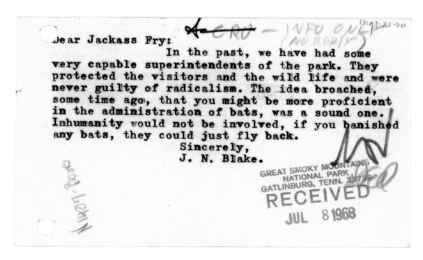

Public outrage over the proposed bear-management program manifested itself in hate mail like this postcard and that on page 140 to Superintendent George Fry.

proposed that the names of those cited for feeding wildlife be released to local media.

Two aspects of the program, however, proved highly controversial— bear removal and aversion therapy. According to management, on the first appearance of a food-conditioned bear in a campground or along US 441, the bear would be captured and removed to a remote location outside the park boundary. Should a relocated bear return to the park, the decision would be made to either remove the bear again or to euthanize it. The plan also stated: "As soon as the first bear appears in the spring along other sections of roadside, start instilling in them their normal inherent fear of humans." What this involved wasn't precisely spelled out in the policy.

Developing this new program turned out to be much easier than accurately communicating it to the public. As these two postcards addressed to Superintendent Fry demonstrate, the public didn't necessarily embrace the new policy.

The news of the management plan was first reported in the *Knoxville News-Sentinel* on April 21, 1968, and it was here that the turmoil began. According to the article, the plan involved "removing bears on first appearance, from the Chimneys and Elkmont Camp Grounds and along US 441 at park headquarters and Newfound Gap." This led readers to believe that all bears, not just those seeking human food, would be removed from the park.

The article went on to claim that bears would be hit with clubs to instill a fear of humans in them. Management didn't spell out what aversion method would be used, so the source of this information is unclear. Interestingly, the *News-Sentinel* piece was written by Georgianna Fry, daughter of Superintendent Fry. Could an off-hand comment at home have made it into the published story and created a colossal misunderstanding?

Subsequent newspaper articles only added fuel to the fire. Walter Amann, an outdoor writer for the *Knoxville Record*, called the plan "a diabolical scheme to rid Smoky Park of native black bears" and encouraged his readers to write letters of complaint to their elected officials. He opined that if enough people complained perhaps Fry would be removed to a park that had only caves and hibernating bats. Private citizens, elected officials, and even members of conservation organizations seemed eager to accept poor reporting and wild rumor rather than the park's actual policy.

In one instance, 18 faculty members of the Department of Psychology at the University of Tennessee signed a letter questioning the counterconditioning methods proposed. They feared that the policy of "hitting bears with clubs to train them to be afraid of humans" could in fact encourage bears to be more aggressive to humans. Believing that all bears would be removed from the park, a member of the North Carolina Department of Conservation and Development expressed fears that the state would suffer the loss of tourist dollars. People wrote to their state and national representatives, the Secretary of the Interior, and even Lady Bird Johnson to express their outrage. To make matters worse, Fry allowed himself to be drawn into a rather lengthy correspondence with a local resident that can best be characterized as snarky and condescending.

The adverse publicity, however, did nothing to sway park management from its decision. The plan was implemented with the full support of officials in Washington. The following year the number of bear incidents was reduced drastically from previous years.

One of the most important, but at the time overlooked, aspects of the plan was the systematic study of the Smokies' black bear population. In the years to follow, an extensive study of black bear and human interaction would result in a greater emphasis on the impact of human activities on bear behavior. In 1976, a new bear-management policy was released that shifted the focus toward visitor education and away from "hitting bears with clubs." ∾

NOTICE TO BEARS

Beware of Sabotage

We want to warn you that certain humans in this park have been passing the biscuits and soda pop to some of your brothers. Keep your self-respect—avoid them. Don't be pauperized like your uncles were last year. You remember what happened to those panhandlers, don't you?

Do you want gout, an unbalanced diet, vitamin deficiencies, or gas on the stomach? Beware of "ersatz" foodstuffs—accept only natural foods and hunt these up yourself.

These visitors mean well but they will ignore the signs. If they come too close, read this notice to them. They'll catch on after awhile.

THE COMMITTEE.

If you can't read, ask the bear at the next intersection.

GPO   16—40700-1

The National Park Service employed different methods to educate the public about the hazards of feeding bears, including messages that were humorous and some that were sobering.

Bibliography

EARLY DOCUMENTS OF THE GREAT SMOKY
MOUNTAINS, 1785–1879

Franklin, the State That Never Was

Barksdale, Kevin T. *The Lost State of Franklin: America's First Secession.* Lexington, University Press of Kentucky, 2008.

Foster, Dave. *Franklin: The Stillborn State and the Sevier/Tipton Political Feud.* Johnson City, Tennessee: Overmountain Press, 2003.

Irwin, Ned. "The Lost Papers of the 'Lost State of Franklin.'" *Journal of East Tennessee History* 69 (1997): 84–96.

Williams, Samuel Cole. *History of the Lost State of Franklin.* New York: Press of the Pioneers, 1924.

Grievous to Posterity: Enslavement in Southern Appalachia

Allen, W. C. *Annals of Haywood County, North Carolina, 1808–1935: Historical, Sociological, Biographical and Genealogical.* 1935. Reprint, Morgantown, PA: Higginson Book Company, 1977.

The Black Community History Project. Black in Appalachia. https://blackinappalachia.omeka.net.

Blackmun, Ora. *Western North Carolina: Its Mountains and Its People to 1880*. Boone, NC: Appalachian Consortium Press, 1977.

Cutshall, Katherine Calhoun. "In the Grip of Slavery: The Rise of a Slave Society Surrounding the Establishment of Stock Stands along the Buncombe Turnpike, 1790 to 1855." Thesis, University of North Carolina Asheville, 2015.

Digital Library on American Slavery. University of North Carolina Greensboro. https://dlas.uncg.edu.

Inscoe, John C. *Mountain Masters: Slavery and the Sectional Crisis in Western North Carolina*. Knoxville: University of Tennessee Press, 1989.

Medford, W. Clark. *The Early History of Haywood County*. Asheville, NC: Miller, 1961.

Olmsted, Frederick Law. *A Journey in the Seaboard Slave States: With Remarks on Their Economy*. New York: G.P. Putnam and Sons, 1904.

———. *The Cotton Kingdom: A Traveller's Observations on Cotton and Slavery in the American Slave States, 1853–1861*. New York: Mason Brothers, 1861.

United States Bureau of the Census. *Fifth Census of the United States*, 1830. *Sixth Census of the United States*, 1840. *Seventh Census of the United States*, 1850. *Eighth Census of the United States*, 1860. *Ninth Census of the United States*, 1870. National Archives and Records Administration. https://archives.gov.

Faithful Observance: Elijah Oliver, Cades Cove, and the Civil War

Dunn, Durwood. *Cades Cove: The Life and Death of a Southern Appalachian Community, 1818–1937*. Knoxville: University of Tennessee Press, 1988.

Fisher, Noel. *The Civil War in the Smokies*. Gatlinburg, TN: Great Smoky Mountains Association, 2005.

Groce, W. Todd. *Mountain Rebels: East Tennessee Confederates and the Civil War, 1860–1870*. Knoxville: University of Tennessee Press, 1999.

Oliver, W. H. "Sketches of the Olivers." Unpublished manuscript, 1931–32. Great Smoky Mountains National Park Archives.

Into the Unknown Sea of Freedom

Alexander, Roberta Sue. "Hostility and Hope: Black Education in North Carolina during Presidential Reconstruction, 1865–1867." *North Carolina Historical Review* 53, no. 2 (April 1976): 113–32.

"Black and African American Genealogy." Western Carolina University, Hunter Library, research guide. https://researchguides.wcu.edu/Genealogy/BlackAnddAfricanAmerican.

Nash, Steven E. *Reconstruction's Ragged Edge: The Politics of Postwar Life in the Southern Mountains.* Chapel Hill: University of North Carolina Press, 2016.

"Records for the Field Offices for the State of North Carolina, Bureau of Refugees, Freedmen, and Abandoned Lands, 1865–1872, Asheville." Freedmen's Bureau Preservation Project. Washington, DC: United States Congress and National Archives and Records Administration, 2004. https://archives.gov/files/research/microfilm/m1909.pdf.

Savage, Kirk. "A Personal Act of Reparation: The Long Aftermath of a North Carolina Man's Decision to Deed a Plot of Land to His Former Slaves." *Lapham's Quarterly*, December 15, 2019. https://www.laphamsquarterly.org/roundtable/personal-act-reparation.

"Slavery, Abolition, Emancipation and Freedom: Primary Sources from Houghton Library." Harvard University, Houghton Library, digital collection. https://curiosity.lib.harvard.edu/slavery-abolition-emancipation-and-freedom.

Van Noppen, Ina Woestemeyer. *Western North Carolina Since the Civil War.* Boone, NC: Appalachian Consortium Press, 1973.

Such a Charming Writer: Mary Noailles Murfree

Abramson, Rudy and Jean Haskell, eds. *Encyclopedia of Appalachia.* Knoxville: University of Tennessee Press, 2006.

Byer, James E. "Legendary Places: The Literature of the Great Smoky Mountains National Park." *Journal of the Appalachian Studies Association* 1, no. 1 (1989): 46–54.

Charles Egbert Craddock Papers. Great Smoky Mountains National Park Archives.

Ensor, Allison. "Mary Noailles Murfree ('Charles Egbert Craddock')." *The Tennessee Encyclopedia.* https://tennesseeencyclopedia.net/entries/mary-noailles-murfree.

Tucker, Edward L. "A Letter by Mary Noailles Murfree." *Mississippi Quarterly* 56, no. 1 (Winter 2002–03): 147–50.

Accounting for a Life

Allen, W. C. *Annals of Haywood County, North Carolina, 1808–1935: Historical, Sociological, Biographical and Genealogical.* 1935. Reprint, Morgantown, PA: Higginson Book Company, 1977.

Blackmun, Ora. *Western North Carolina: Its Mountains and Its People to 1880.* Boone, NC: Appalachian Consortium Press, 1977.

Hornsby-Gutting, Angela M. "Manning the Region: New Approaches to Gender in the South." *Journal of Southern History* 63, no. 3 (August 2009): 663–76.

Medford, W. Clark. *The Early History of Haywood County.* Asheville, NC: Miller, 1961.

Van Noppen, Ina Woestemeyer. *Western North Carolina Since the Civil War.* Boone, NC: Appalachian Consortium Press, 1973.

"Women Postmasters." United States Postal Service. Updated February 2021. https://about.usps.com/who-we-are/postal-history/women-postmasters.pdf.

A Blizzard of Limericks

Campbell, Carlos. *Birth of a National Park in the Great Smoky Mountains*. Knoxville: University of Tennessee Press, 1993.

———. *Memories of Old Smoky: Early Experiences in the Great Smoky Mountains*. Knoxville: University of Tennessee Press, 2005.

The Carlos Campbell Collection. Great Smoky Mountains National Park Archives.

Anne Davis, for the Park and the People

Catton, Theodore. *Mountains for the Masses: A History of Management Issues in Great Smoky Mountains National Park*. Gatlinburg: Great Smoky Mountains Association, 2014.

Pierce, Dan S. *Great Smokies: From Natural Habitat to National Park*. Knoxville: University of Tennessee Press, 2015.

Willis P. and Anne Davis Collection. Great Smoky Mountains National Park Archives.

A Troubled Compromise

Jones, Rebecca. *Historic Resource Study: African Americans and the Blue Ridge Parkway* (n.p.: National Park Service, 2009). http://npshistory.com/publications/blri/hrs-african-americans.pdf.

O'Brien, William E. "State Parks and Jim Crow in the Decade before Brown v. Board of Education." *Geographical Review* 102, no. 2. (2012): 166–79. https://www.jstor.org/stable/41709174.

Resource Management Records. Office of the Superintendent. Great Smoky Mountains National Park Archives.

Scott, David, and Kang Jae Jerry Lee. "People of Color and Their Constraints to National Parks Visitation." *The George Wright Forum* 35, no. 1 (2018): 73–82. https://www.jstor.org/stable/26452993.

Shumaker, Susan. "Segregation in the National Parks, 1870s–1964." *Untold Stories from America's National Parks.* 1:15–36. Boston: Public Broadcasting Service, 2004. https://www.pbs.org/kenburns/the-national-parks/.

Thom El-Amin, Enkeshi. "Chocolate City Way Up South in Appalachia: Black Knoxville at the Intersection of Race, Place, and Region." PhD diss., University of Tennessee, 2019. https://trace.tennessee.edu/utk_graddiss/5340/.

Young, Terence. *Heading Out: A History of American Camping.* Ithaca, NY: Cornell University Press, 2017.

Bob and Calvin's Big Adventure

Catton, Theodore. *Mountains for the Masses: A History of Management Issues in Great Smoky Mountains National Park.* Gatlinburg: Great Smoky Mountains Association, 2014.

Great Smoky Mountains Conservation Association Collection. Great Smoky Mountains National Park Archives.

Help Us, Rockefeller, You're Our Only Hope!

Catton, Theodore. *Mountains for the Masses: A History of Management Issues in Great Smoky Mountains National Park.* Gatlinburg: Great Smoky Mountains Association, 2014.

The David Chapman Collection. Great Smoky Mountains National Park Archives.

Dunn, Durwood. *Cades Cove: The Life and Death of a Southern Appalachian Community, 1818–1937.* Knoxville: University of Tennessee Press, 1988.

Great Smoky Mountains Conservation Association Collection. Great Smoky Mountains National Park Archives.

Harp Singing and Squirrel Stew

Catton, Theodore. *Mountains for the Masses: A History of Management Issues in Great Smoky Mountains National Park*. Gatlinburg: Great Smoky Mountains Association, 2014.

Myers, Bonnie Trentham. *The Walker Sisters: Spirited Women of the Smokies*. Maryville, TN: Myers and Myers, 2004.

Walker, Melissa. *All We Knew Was to Farm: Rural Women in the Upcountry South, 1919–1941*. Baltimore: Johns Hopkins University Press, 2000.

Walker Sisters Papers. Great Smoky Mountains National Park Archives.

CHRONICLES OF A YOUNG NATIONAL PARK IN THE SMOKIES, 1935–1968

The Tragic Death of Charles Maner

Catton, Theodore. *Mountains for the Masses: A History of Management Issues in Great Smoky Mountains National Park*. Gatlinburg: Great Smoky Mountains Association, 2014.

Civilian Conservation Corp (CCC) Collection. Great Smoky Mountains National Park Archives.

Paige, John C. *The Civilian Conservation Corps and the National Park Service, 1933–1942: An Administrative History*. Washington, DC: National Park Service, 1985. http://npshistory.com/publications/ccc/adhi-ccc.pdf.

A Proposal for Cades Cove Lake

Catton, Theodore. *Mountains for the Masses: A History of Management Issues in Great Smoky Mountains National Park*. Gatlinburg: Great Smoky Mountains Association, 2014.

Great Smoky Mountains Conservation Association Collection. Great Smoky Mountains National Park Archives.

"Thou Noest That Times Is Hard"

Brown, Margaret Lynn. *The Wild East: A Biography of the Great Smoky Mountains.* Gainesville: University Press of Florida, 2000.

Catton, Theodore. *Mountains for the Masses: A History of Management Issues in Great Smoky Mountains National Park.* Gatlinburg: Great Smoky Mountains Association, 2014.

Great Smoky Mountains Conservation Association Collection. Great Smoky Mountains National Park Archives.

Such Sunsets Out of Our Windows

Blaylock, Matthew Robert. "Appalachian Aristocrats: How Tourists, Elites, and Mountaineers Created a New Western North Carolina, 1880–1920." PhD diss., University of Tennessee, 2017. https://trace.tennessee.edu/utk_graddiss/4680/.

Martin, C. Brenden, *Tourism in the Mountain South: A Double-Edged Sword.* Knoxville: University of Tennessee Press, 2007.

Shaffer, Marguerite. *See America First, Tourism and National Identity, 1880–1940.* Washington, DC: Smithsonian Institution Press, 2001.

Balancing Act on Mount Le Conte

Catton, Theodore. *Mountains for the Masses: A History of Management Issues in Great Smoky Mountains National Park.* Gatlinburg: Great Smoky Mountains Association, 2014.

Resource Management Records. Central File. Great Smoky Mountains National Park Archives.

Two for the Road

Arthur Stupka Collection. Great Smoky Mountains National Park Archives.

Peterson, Roger Tory, and James Fisher. *Wild America: The Legendary Story of Two Great Naturalists on the Road.* 1955. Reprint, Boston: Houghton Mifflin, 1997.

A Plan to Beat and Banish Bears

Catton, Theodore. *Mountains for the Masses: A History of Management Issues in Great Smoky Mountains National Park*. Gatlinburg: Great Smoky Mountains Association, 2014.

Madison, Joseph S. "Yosemite National Park: The Continuous Evolution of Human-Black Bear Conflict Management." *Human–Wildlife Conflicts* 2, no. 2 (Fall 2008): 160–67.

Resource Management Records. Resource Management Division. Great Smoky Mountains National Park Archives.

Resource Management Records. Visitor and Resource Protection Division. Great Smoky Mountains National Park Archives.

Smith, Emily E. "The Deadly Grizzly Bear Attacks That Changed the National Park Service Forever." *Smithsonian Magazine*, August 10, 2017. https://www.smithsonianmag.com/history/deadly-grizzly-bear-attacks-changed-national-park-service-forever-180964462/.

Index

Page numbers followed by *"fig."* refer to illustrations and their captions.
Page numbers followed by *"n."* refer to notes.

155

About the Author

Mike Aday is the librarian-archivist at Great Smoky Mountains National Park. Originally from Texas, Mike earned a master's degree in history and archival administration from the University of Texas at Arlington. He has worked in numerous cultural resource repositories, including the Dallas Municipal Archives, the Dallas Museum of Art, and the Old Red Museum of Dallas County History and Culture.

In 2012, Mike and his wife, Denise, sold almost everything they owned; put two cats, two suitcases, and seven boxes in their Mazda Protégé; and moved to Yosemite National Park, where Mike began a one-year term as an archives technician.

In 2013, the Adays moved from California to Pigeon Forge, Tennessee, where Mike took over management of the Smokies archives. Since then, he has helped thousands of researchers uncover the history of the park, the region, and its people. He has also contributed to *Smokies Life* journal and the Smokies LIVE blog.

Mike and Denise now live in Maryville, Tennessee. They enjoy exploring all that Southern Appalachia has to offer. ❧